VIEWING OLMSTED

PHOTOGRAPHS BY ROBERT BURLEY, LEE FRIEDLANDER,

AND GEOFFREY JAMES

VIEWING OLMSTED

PHOTOGRAPHS BY

ROBERT BURLEY

LEE FRIEDLANDER

AND

GEOFFREY JAMES

EDITED BY PHYLLIS LAMBERT

CENTRE CANADIEN D'ARCHITECTURE /
CANADIAN CENTRE FOR ARCHITECTURE, MONTRÉAL

DISTRIBUTED BY THE MIT PRESS, CAMBRIDGE, MASSACHUSETTS, AND LONDON, ENGLAND

Published in conjunction with the exhibition *Viewing Olmsted: Photographs by Robert Burley, Lee Friedlander, and Geoffrey James*, presented at the Canadian Centre for Architecture (CCA), Montréal, from 16 October 1996 to 2 February 1997, the Equitable Gallery, New York City, from 12 February to 15 March 1997, the Wexner Center for the Arts, Columbus, Ohio, from 9 May to 10 August 1997, and the Davis Museum Center, Wellesley, Massachusetts, from 2 September to 23 November 1997. David Harris, supervisor of the commission, is the curator for the exhibition.

This publication has been supported by grants from the Graham Foundation for Advanced Studies in the Fine Arts and *Furthermore*... the J. M. Kaplan Fund publication program. The CCA gratefully acknowledges the J. W. McConnell Family Foundation, Daniel Langlois, Hydro-Québec, and Matthew Bronfman and Lisa Belzberg for gifts in support of the exhibition and its accompanying educational programs.

The CCA also acknowledges the support of the Museums Assistance Program of the Department of Canadian Heritage, the Canada Council, the Ministère de la Culture et des Communications du Québec, the Conseil des arts de la Communauté urbaine de Montréal, and the Service de la culture de la Ville de Montréal for the exhibition and the accompanying educational programs.

The CCA benefits from the operating support of the Ministère de la Culture et des Communications du Québec and the Conseil des arts de la Communauté urbaine de Montréal.

Legal Deposit
Bibliothèque nationale du Québec, 1996
National Library of Canada, 1996

Printed in Canada

CCA ISBN 0-920785-58-1
MIT ISBN 0-262-62116-9
Library of Congress Card Number 96-79062

CANADIAN CATALOGUING IN PUBLICATION DATA
Main entry under title:
Viewing Olmsted: photographs
Catalogue of an exhibition held at Canadian Centre for Architecture, Montréal, Oct. 16 1996–Feb. 2nd 1997.
ISBN 0-920785-58-1
1. Olmsted, Frederick Law, 1822–1903 – Exhibitions. 2. Burley, Robert – Exhibitions. 3. Friedlander, Lee – Exhibitions. 4. James, Geoffrey – Exhibitions. 5. Parks in art – Exhibitions. 6. Landscape photography – Exhibitions. I. Lambert, Phyllis. II. Burley, Robert, 1957– . III. Friedlander, Lee, 1934– . IV. James, Geoffrey, 1942– . V. Canadian Centre for Architecture.
SB470.05V53 1996 712.092 C96-941338-6

Photographs
Portfolio plates and cover, CCA Photographic Services; fig. 1, The Museum of Modern Art, New York; fig. 2, The Century Association, New York; figs. 3 and 4, photographs by Ansel Adams

Distributed by The MIT Press, Cambridge, Massachusetts, and London, England

Senior Editor: Christine Dufresne
Production Editor: Denis Hunter
Editor: Marcia Rodríguez
Design: Katy Homans
Reproduction rights: Jocelyne Gervais

Front cover
Lee Friedlander, *Franklin Park, Boston, Massachusetts*, 1994. Gelatin silver print, 33.8 x 13.8 cm. CCA PH1994:0173

Back cover
Above: Geoffrey James, *Charlestown Heights, Boston, Massachusetts*, 1994. Gelatin silver print, 19.5 x 24.5 cm. CCA PH1994:0081
Below: Lee Friedlander, *Charlestown Heights, Boston, Massachusetts*, 1994. Gelatin silver print, 26.5 x 26 cm. CCA PH1994:0177
Right: Robert Burley, *Charlestown Heights, Boston, Massachusetts*, 1994. Chromogenic colour print, 23.2 x 30.1 cm. CCA PH1994:0035

CONTENTS

The Centre Canadien d'Architecture/Canadian Centre for Architecture (CCA) is a study centre and a museum devoted to the art of architecture and its history. It is founded on the conviction that architecture, as part of the social and natural environment, is a public concern. The CCA's activities are international in scope and are based on a unique collection of works of art and documentation from all areas – architecture, urban planning, and landscape design – that are part of the built environment.

PROLOGUE

What artist so noble, as he, who, with far-reaching conception of beauty and designing-power, sketches the outlines, writes the colors, and directs the shadows, of a picture so great that Nature shall be employed upon it for generations, before the work he has arranged for her shall realize his intentions.

FREDERICK LAW OLMSTED[1]

After a hundred years we have reached the time by which Frederick Law Olmsted considered his landscapes would have matured. Did he mean the work of Nature alone? Did he include the social landscapes of the parks? And the form of the city around them?

Changes over time are inherent in the photographs in the Olmsted commission – splendid century-old specimen trees, the scruffy rows of saplings recently planted to transform greenswards into golf links, a newly tarred roadway stopping abruptly along the slope of another vast swath of green. Close viewing will reveal a distant crowd, leaving, perhaps, a baseball game or a football field. In some images the roar of traffic can be sensed above the sound of water in a swift stream; elsewhere, a chain-link fence creates a barrier edge for joggers who round a reservoir, or wards off an intruding highway. Old masonry walls crumble while parapet walls, skilfully carved statues, or cast-iron railings remain. Buildings have outstripped the tallest trees of Central Park and in the same way densely packed buildings below Montréal's mountain remind us how relentless the city grid would have been without the vast, civilizing Olmsted parks.

The enormous physical and social changes that have obtained in North American cities over the course of this century have been encompassed by the photographers of *Viewing Olmsted*, not overtly, but in their search to understand the palpable experience of Olmsted's landscape that has been the foreground of their work. To that extent this book is about phenomenology, the external space we grasp through our bodily situation. In the act of photographing, painting, observing, "the body is much more than an instrument or a means; it is our expression in the world, the visible form of our intentions. Even our most secret affective movements, those most deeply tied to the humoral infrastructure, help to shape our perception of things."[2] For the leading phenomenologist of the twentieth century, Maurice Merleau-Ponty (1908–1961), order is made out of disorder by our ability to give meaning to our experience, and leads to another form of knowledge, the perception of objects through the animation of the body by the soul, an activity "long considered by philosophy to be pure knowledge."[3]

Considering art, Merleau-Ponty quotes Valéry: "The painter takes his body with him." "Indeed," he continues, "we cannot imagine how a *mind* could paint. It is by lending his body to the world that the artist changes the world into paintings. To understand these transubstantiations we must go back to the working, actual body – not the body as a chunk of space or a bundle of functions, but that body which is an intertwining of vision and movement."[4] In *Viewing Olmsted*, over the seven years of learning to understand his landscape, the body has been central to the experience of the photographers in absorbing its essence, propelling them onward from place to place, compelling them to stop, to observe, to set up, to point, to make a subtle move, to make an image. The phenomenon of the educated eye sees light against dark, volume against line.

We in turn learn to read the images and to become aware not only of the art of Olmsted but the art of each photographer as he has come to view Olmsted over time. Through Robert Burley we are aware of people, how they occupy space, knowingly observed yet isolated in the magic that a place lends to their private world. With Geoffrey James we follow Olmsted's path through grand sweeps of space defined by the placement of trees and the swell of the landforms designed to lead one on. We are corporeally engaged by the intimacy of Lee Friedlander's tactile sense and complexity of image – the landscape's tangled edges, the texture of leaves, bared branches, roots, trunks, shadows, the persona of a tree. In all the images we sense the seasons, the mood of the land, and the struggle each photographer had not to copy, not to offer things to thought as does science, but by attending to surfaces and the structures beneath them to render elements "no longer visible in their own right, but [that] rather contribute as they do in natural vision, to the impression of an emerging order, of an object in the act of appearing, organizing itself before our eyes," as Merleau-Ponty wrote of Cézanne.[5]

Space and time are also part of the process. The sense of time is not only of the land, but within each photographer's oeuvre. "As a result of being able to return to a number of parks over a period of years," Robert Burley notes in this volume, "I found that they were constantly reinvented places, not just through the change of seasons and the different activities that took place there, but through Olmsted's design skills. He was someone who really had an immense talent for manipulating not only the landscape but the way people experienced it. Being a picture-maker, one tries to be aware of how people view your pictures and how you can manipulate their eye around an image. Olmsted, as someone who created landscapes, was incredibly successful at manipulating me in a very deliberate way around his landscapes. Even when I was very much aware of it, and even when I tried to find alternative routes, I found myself following a kind of itinerary that I think he had probably developed."

Geoffrey James also draws a parallel between Olmsted's crafting of space and the work of the photographer: "I learned that before you can make a picture, you have to find the spot, and you find the spot by walking. There is a walking activity with the machine and you are not peering through it – you are sort of sniffing, you are like a dog, trying to find the right spot. It is very, very instinctive. There were certain places that seemed to me had been designed, were consciously designed, to make you do this walk, to move your body through the space. There is . . . a journey to be made, almost a narrative."

The challenge of rendering the implied movement within these spaces, the continual changing of the landscape with the seasons and the weather, the sheer size of the places, leads to an interpretation from multiple, overlapping points of view. In the words of Lee Friedlander, "I don't think anyone is capable of doing the definitive Central Park. In some ways we all – Bob and Geoffrey and myself – probably felt a relief, thinking, if I didn't get it somebody else did. Going out with those guys was fun because the ironies were just so hilarious. I could go out with them and you could almost have tied us so we were back to back, and one of us could be totally interested in one area and the other one the complete opposite. It was really funny that could happen. I don't think any of us who went out together were ever interested in the same thing."

The photographer's gaze partakes of Olmsted's intensity of observation and ability to synthesize experience. These qualities Olmsted brought to the profession of landscape design which he entered at age thirty-five, when he and the British architect Calvert Vaux won the competition to design New York's Central Park. Olmsted's early years as a farmer first in Connecticut and then on Staten Island, New York, developed his knowledge of the technicalities of land management, especially of wetlands, which has given enduring stability and health to the former swamplands of Boston he fashioned into the Fens, and to the marshes of the island of Manhattan he transformed into Central Park.

Olmsted's travels in Europe convinced him that the picturesque places of North America must be kept open as public land rather than privately maintained by and for the economically privileged, as he had found abroad. Indeed, his visits to the famous gardens of England and his knowledge of the related literature heightened his sensibilities toward the aesthetics of the picturesque. Yet I wonder whether his compositional strengths, which the photographers sought to capture, do not derive from the late-nineteenth-century principles of design established by the École des Beaux-Arts, with its canonic progression through contrasting space. In a collage of the photographs made in Olmsted's parks, we sense the classical Beaux-Arts progression from expansive, high, bright spaces to darker confining ones, mediated by constricting passages. In his parks one moves from the greensward open to the sky through the confines of a tunnel or a bridge, into the penumbra of a deep space, "an open grove of forest trees, in which visitors may ramble in the shade without impediment of underwood."[6]

Olmsted designed each site for a variety of uses, requiring only that the new features harmonize with the natural appearance of the landscape. Driveways, walks, playgrounds, bodies of water, rocky outcroppings, greenswards, and meadows with native forest trees were all integral to Olmsted's conception of these places as public facilities, "so as to admit of the amplest development of individuals, which will be further encouraged by the best attainable conditions of soil and situation."[7] Artifice would transform raw cuts for roadways by shaping banks "in such desirable forms as frost, and rain, and root growths might chance to give them after many years. You can do more. You can, by a little forecast, make them at one point bolder, and more picturesque in contour by a fitting buttress of rock, than nature, working alone would be able to do."[8] In planting trees he provided both canopy and shadow, and, this being done, kept the abrupt bank from eroding.

Olmsted's concern for the ecological aspects of design and longevity was continuous, fundamental. "The only way in which any town park can long be kept in a generally useful and improving condition, is by providing so well and amply for the uses which are designed to be made of it that the great body of decent, orderly, tidy, and respectable people will not be impelled to fall into practices inconvenient to others or unfavorable to the preservation and improvement of its natural beauty."[9] For much of this century, little attention was paid to Olmsted's achievement, and the sites he designed, particularly public parks, were unattended to. In the 1960s, however, they became part of a public consciousness with the beginning of the environmental and urban preservation movements. A new generation has seen the creation of the Frederick Law Olmsted National Historic Site, which has provided base documentation for the restoration of Olmsted sites throughout North America, none more systematically than the Management and Restoration Plan of the New York City Department of Parks and Restoration together with the Central Park Conservancy, a private agency. And these concerns of Olmsted's form another layer imbued in the photographs, consciously or unconsciously. Geoffrey James, in particular, hoped that his work would help to inspire care of the landscape.

Like grains of sand that can be sorted according to size, colour, form, density, geological composition, time, and the action of the sea, *Viewing Olmsted* leads to a critical social, economic, and architectural reading of Olmsted's work and its legacy, and overarching readings of time and the phenomenology of space.

The photographic mission was inherent in the great art form developed by Louis Jacques Mandé Daguerre and William Henry Fox Talbot less than a generation before Olmsted's design of Central Park. The multiplicity of views it allows is one of the defining aspects of modernity. This new art form privileged images organized in sequence, or collaged, superposed, and variably recomposed, which, like the parks, one might apprehend as a whole.

The images of *Viewing Olmsted* give access to the pleasure to be had in subtle ways of looking at and immersing oneself in landscape. At the same time they provoke reflection on the other ways in which we can view the landscape of our towns: the role of the citizen in maintaining and protecting this legacy and the social, physical, and political structures that can replace the citizen body as central to our cities.

* * *

For their contribution to the project, I wish to thank the photographers Robert Burley, Lee Friedlander, and Geoffrey James; the historian Cynthia Zaitzevsky, who selected the sites in the commission; John Szarkowski, Director Emeritus of the Department of Photography of The Museum of Modern Art, New York, who contributed an essay to this volume; Katy Homans, designer of the book; and, at the CCA, Paolo Costantini, Curator, Photographs Collection; David Harris, who supervised the commission and curated the exhibition; and Gwendolyn Owens, Assistant Director, Museum Services.

The exhibition, its accompanying educational programs, and the publication of this book have been kindly supported by the J. W. McConnell Family Foundation, Daniel Langlois, the Graham Foundation for Advanced Studies in the Fine Arts, *Furthermore...* the J. M. Kaplan Fund publication program, Hydro-Québec, and Matthew Bronfman and Lisa Belzberg. We are grateful also to the Museums Assistance Program of the Department of Canadian Heritage, the Canada Council, the Ministère de la Culture et des Communications du Québec, the Conseil des arts de la Communauté urbaine de Montréal, and the Service de la culture de la Ville de Montréal, who have given generous support to the exhibition and its educational programs. The CCA benefits from the operating support of the Ministère de la Culture et des Communications du Québec and the Conseil des arts de la Communauté urbaine de Montréal.

PHYLLIS LAMBERT

DIRECTOR, CCA

1. Olmsted notes that "thirty years ago, before the Park was dreamed of, as a farmer, and with no more idea that I should ever be a professional landscape-designer than that I should command a fleet, I had printed these thoroughly unpractical words. . . ." "Frederick Law Olmsted: The Spoils of the Park: With a Few Leaves from the Deep-laden Note-books of a 'Wholly Unpractical Man,'" in Albert Fein, ed., *Landscape Into Cityscape: Frederick Law Olmsted's Plans for a Greater New York City* (Ithaca, 1967), 427.

2. Maurice Merleau-Ponty, "An Unpublished Text by Maurice Merleau-Ponty: A Prospectus of his Work," translated by Arleen B. Dallery, in Maurice Merleau-Ponty, *The Primacy of Perception and Other Essays on Phenomenological Psychology, the Philosophy of Art, History, and Politics*, ed. James M. Edie (Evanston, 1964), 5. This text, which was included in Merleau-Ponty's papers as part of his candidacy to the Collège de France, was published in the *Revue de Métaphysique et de Morale* in 1962.

3. Merleau-Ponty, *The Primacy of Perception*, 5.

4. Merleau-Ponty, "Eye and Mind," translated by Carleton Dallery, in *The Primacy of Perception*, 162.

5. Merleau-Ponty, "Cézanne's Doubt," in *Sense and Non-sense*, translated by H. L. Dreyfus and P. A. Dreyfus (Evanston, 1964), quoted by John J. Compton, in David E. Cooper, ed., *A Companion to Aesthetics* (Oxford, 1992), 284.

6. Frederick Law Olmsted and Calvert Vaux, "Preliminary Report to the Commissioners for Laying Out a Park in Brooklyn, New York," 1866, in Fein, *Landscape Into Cityscape*, 113.

7. Olmsted and Vaux, "Preliminary Report," 113.

8. Frederick Law Olmsted, *Mount Royal, Montreal* (New York, 1881), 33.

9. Olmsted, *Mount Royal*, 53.

AN ARCHAEOLOGIST'S VISION

PAOLO COSTANTINI

The idea of a photographic commission on the work of Frederick Law Olmsted dates back to October 1987, when the photographer Geoffrey James proposed an extensive, multilayered photographic exploration of the present state of the parks conceived, designed, and realized by Olmsted in North America. Implicit in such a project was the chance to reflect not only on the subtle dialectic between past and present, on the subsequent transformations in the complex environmental systems that Olmsted had fashioned, but on the very idea of the "park" and its significance within a profoundly changed society.

This initial idea developed into the most important photographic commission that the CCA has yet undertaken. It falls within a larger, wide-ranging inquiry currently engaged in by the CCA, the critical rethinking of the cultural impact of certain issues associated with the *American Century*. In this context, the project assumes a greater importance as part of a richly interwoven and deeply textured architectural culture in which Olmsted figures within the ongoing dialogue between landscape and city – the same dialogue occasioned by Frank Lloyd Wright in his work of the 1920s, by the emblematic role of the American lawn in civic and social life, and by Europe's perception of the transformations wrought on the American city at the beginning of the twentieth century.[1]

The Olmsted project involved the participation of three photographers: Lee Friedlander, a preeminent observer and investigator of the American social landscape; Geoffrey James, well known for his photographic studies of European gardens; and a young architectural photographer working in colour, Robert Burley. The photographers were left entirely free to pursue their visual exploration within each site without being assigned specific territories or distinct themes. The object was to experiment with a multiplicity of approaches and points of view.

Given the complexity of themes that such a survey of Olmsted's parks necessarily implied – their widely scattered geographic locations across a vast territory; the survival of many of the original design features within spaces that have undergone gradual transformations in their patterns of use; the relationships between the parks and the cities that contain them; and the different value that such large, planned spaces have today in a radically altered cultural and social context – only a patient and persistent revisiting of these places by the three photographers would allow their readings to respond adequately to their questions, as they developed over time.

Hence Friedlander, James, and Burley had the rare opportunity to "construct" their individual visions over an extended period, through repeated visits and new encounters (sometimes after many years), and through an ongoing re-examination of their own photographic methods, and the geographic and conceptual limits by which each measures his own work. They were also able to discover that working over such a long period of time on a commission meant creating a new context for their images – organizing those they had completed while planning to revisit the sites, renewing their own vision, always ready to add or to make changes and adjustments. This also meant letting other readings emerge, to speak for themselves. The new meanings, as they were encountered in the course of the work, gradually established themselves as essential avenues of inquiry, allowing the photographers to reach more articulate and diverse levels of precision. Finally, it meant accepting and embracing the idea that an analysis of these Olmsted spaces (and, as Freud made clear, any form of analysis) is by its very nature endless, a fact acknowledged by the photographers themselves in the excerpts from the interviews contained in this volume.

The result is not, therefore, a complete, closed, and definitive viewing of Olmsted's work or of his legacy. Rather, it is the record of a seven-year process of discovery, an archive of 936 photographs that make possible a variety of journeys, beginning with those suggested by the images of these photographers. This large corpus of photographs necessarily invites open readings and infinite interpretations. It is as a source for the many reflections to come that this project assumes its greatest importance, and it is in that light that we wish to present it to the public.

The materials in this catalogue and the photographs selected for the exhibition, all from the archive built by the CCA, suggest an important new way of seeing Olmsted's landscapes. From a careful reading of the photographs one can go beyond the desire to observe and record these spaces, toward the deeper desire to actually inhabit them, to guard them against irreparable change, feeling and perceiving them as places that are part of our lives and that, as such, deserve our care and attention.

While the public generally thinks of these spaces as fixed, untouchable, and immutable, they were in fact conceived, designed, and constructed. In the course of the project's seven years, the photographers learned to work with essentially unstable environments that were in constant flux and transformation, aware of the slightest shifts and the most minute alterations. They became increasingly aware of the problematic of such spaces, of the impossibility of ever fully capturing them. Olmsted's parks (as, in fact, are all spaces) are continually being deconstructed, deciphered, and reconquered; they are "fragile" spaces that seem sometimes consumed by time. In this work the photographers have consciously and meticulously sought to arrest something and to help it to survive. They have questioned the complexity of place while at the same time questioning themselves.

If we intend to travel through these landscapes attentively, we must first rediscover the kind of distance that is essential to the exercise of looking, a distance conveyed to us by the photographers who have tried to decipher the spaces that Olmsted mapped. We, like them, can try to see the present from a distance, sometimes with detachment, but always with an attitude that Italo Calvino describes as a "systematic perplexity." Perhaps the best idea is to study both these places and, finally, this archive in an "archaeological" manner, and to adopt, as it seems Friedlander, James, and Burley have done, Calvino's conception of the "archaeologist's vision."

> *We want to make the archaeologist's and the palaeoethnographer's vision our own, turning it not only on the past but also on that layered cross-section that is our own present, and which is strewn with fragmentary and difficult-to-classify human productions.... In his excavations the archaeologist unearths tools about whose use he has no idea, shards of pottery that won't fit together, deposits from eras other than the one he expected to find there: his task is to describe it all piece by piece, and especially*

those things that he has been unable to assign a time or a purpose, or to reconfigure into a continuity or a unity. This may come to him later on, perhaps; or maybe he will understand that all there is to be said comes not from a motivation external to these objects, but from the sole fact that objects like this or like that were found at this or that place.[2]

1. The CCA's multi-year exhibition series *The American Century* casts a fresh eye on critical aspects of modern America's architectural culture – its promises and disappointments, its roots and offshoots, its unparalleled worldwide impact. Other exhibitions in the series are *Scenes of the World to Come: European Architecture and the American Challenge, 1893–1960* (1995), *Frank Lloyd Wright: Designs for an American Landscape, 1922–1932* (1996), *The Architecture of Reassurance: Designing Disney's Theme Parks* (1997), and *The American Lawn: Surface of Everyday Life* (1998).

2 Italo Calvino, "Lo sguardo dell'archeologo" (1972), in *Una pietra sopra: Discorsi di letteratura e società* (Turin, 1990), 263–66.

THE PHOTOGRAPHER IN THE GARDEN

JOHN SZARKOWSKI

André Le Nôtre, chief gardener to Louis XIV, said that he had two million flowerpots at the Grand Trianon, enough to change the colours of the flower beds twice a day (if that were wished). It is a splendid statistic, and proposes a dozen new unanswered questions: how many thousands of assistant gardeners would be required to shuffle two million potted flowers per day; and how many cows would it take, converting grass to manure, to keep the blooms bright and the foliage thrifty; and so forth. But beyond the simple issue of mind-boggling excess, Le Nôtre's comment demonstrates a more interesting point, which is that the gardens of Versailles were never finished.

In fact, one can never say about even the most modest of gardens, *At last! It is finished!* since each of its countless parts is constantly changing, and all of the parts are changing in relation to each other in a way that is – to us, at least – random and inexplicable.

The art of gardening might be thought comparable to the art of the theatre, where some of the component parts of the work are alive, and where every performance is a revision. Or perhaps better and more specifically, the art of gardening might be thought comparable to the art of dance, where impermanence is compounded by systems of notation that are primitive and approximate compared to those for music and spoken drama. But even so, the forces of nature that act to revise the arts of the theatre are the relatively limited forces of human nature, while the art of the gardener is revised also by insects, disease, and the weather.

The arts of the museums change so slowly that we can pretend that they are permanent, but the art of the gardener changes so rapidly and continuously that it is difficult to identify with confidence what the work of art *is*, except to call it a process: a dialogue between the principle of order and the dream of liberty, or (less euphemistically) not a dialogue but a battle – an unequal battle in which order maintains for a time the semblance of equality only by a ceaseless expenditure of money, sweat, and artifice (and perhaps with two million flower pots), while liberty need only bide its time, and wait for civilization to stumble once again.

So if our subject is an idea constantly in the process of disappearing, where should one stand to photograph it?

* * *

The greatest of garden photographers (or park photographers, if you prefer) was the Frenchman Eugène Atget (1857–1927; fig. 1), who habitually stood in very strange places indeed to make his pictures. He almost never pointed his camera on line with the planned *allées* and vistas, since photographs made from such vantage points have no foreground, and seem to have been made from too great a distance by a photographer too tired to get closer. This is an illusion: if the photographer had advanced farther down the *allée* the result would have been much the same, since photography cannot describe space itself. It describes instead objects *in* space, which, because of their size in the picture, we interpret as being at various distances from our vantage point. (The same thing is true of perspective drawing. This is why the figures in quattrocento paintings seem remote from the viewer, and why baroque painters learned to stand in unexpected places, in order to place some figures close to the picture plane, and thus produce more lively pictorial spaces.)

The work of Atget's competitors – like the photographer whose work was published under the firm name "L. P." (fig. 2) – demonstrates the flat and distant effect that results from placing a camera on the expected axis – on the path of the pedestrian visitor. In walking that path, we find the scene altogether satisfactory, but the photograph we make on that line almost always seems empty: a background without a foreground. Atget learned that just as a garden was an artificial reinvention of nature, so was a photograph of a garden a subsequent act of artifice, requiring a reconsideration of the idea in terms of photography's own limitations and potentials: we can photograph a tree, but no breeze will rustle the photograph's leaves, and the birds in its branches will not sing. Nevertheless, if the light and the angle of view and the framing are fortunate, and the technical part of the craft is adequate, then the photograph can make clear some truths about the tree that we would not have recognized in front of the plant itself – distracted perhaps by all the rustling of leaves and the chirping of birds, and by three dimensions.

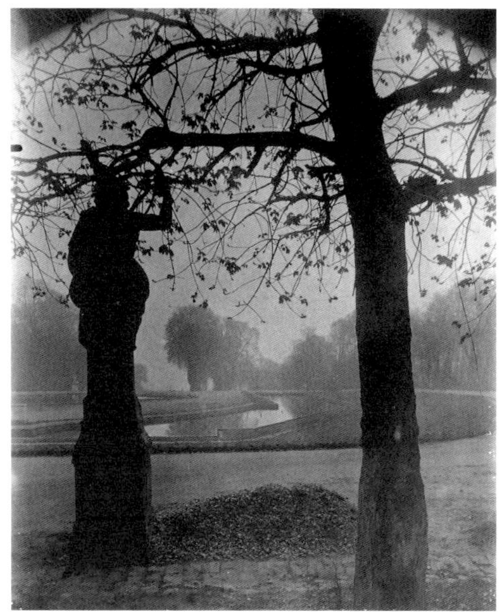

1. Eugène Atget, *Saint-Cloud. 9h. matin, mars 1926*. Plate 83 in *The Ancien Régime*, vol. 3 of *The Work of Atget* (New York, 1984).

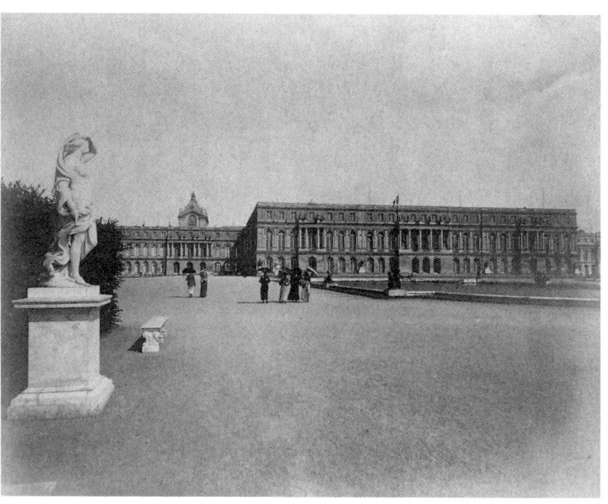

2. L. P. Phot., *Versailles, le château et le parterre d'eau*, no date. Figure 15 in *The Ancien Régime*, vol. 3 of *The Work of Atget* (New York, 1984).

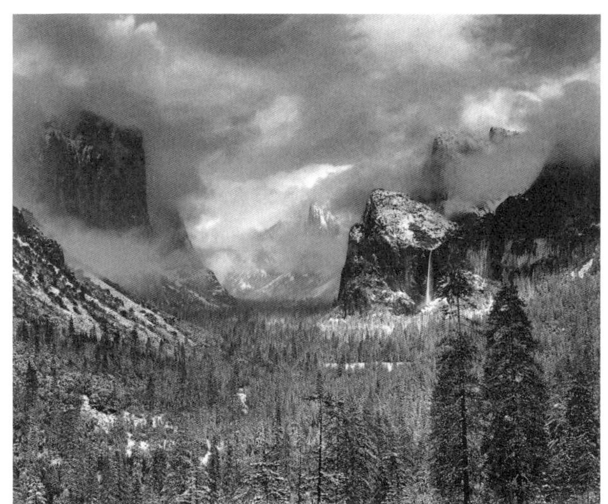

3. Ansel Adams, *Clearing Winter Storm, Yosemite Valley*, 1944. Plate 1 in Ansel Adams, *Yosemite and the Range of Light* (New York, 1979).

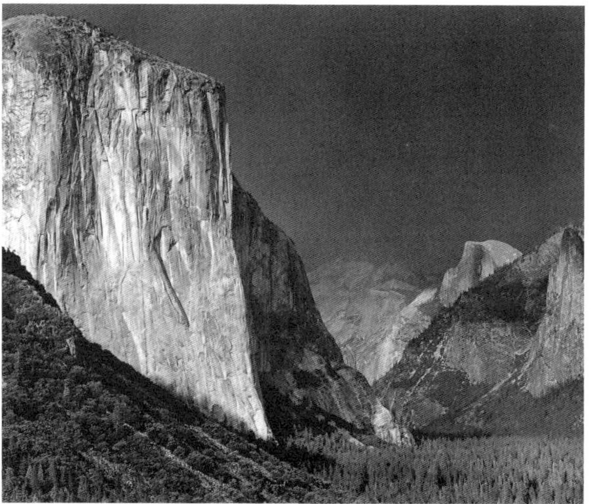

4. Ansel Adams, *El Capitan, Half Dome, Clearing Thunderstorm, Yosemite Valley*, c. 1972. Plate 73 in Ansel Adams, *Yosemite and the Range of Light* (New York, 1979).

Or, alternatively, we might say that the parks of Le Nôtre were based on the idea of absolute authority, and that Atget's great reinterpretation of those places was based on the intuition that they might be reclaimed for the children of the Revolution if the photographer refused to stand on the prescribed authoritarian axes.

* * *

We might compare the problem of photographing a garden (or a park) to the problem of photographing a work of architecture. During the past several generations, students of architecture have (in general) learned most of what they know about the great architectural works of the past not by actually visiting the site (by stagecoach or steam locomotive or on the back of a camel) and then by making sketches and measured drawings, but instead by sitting in a dark room and looking at photographic slides of these monuments. During the past *two* generations, knowledge of contemporary work has also been spread primarily through photographs. In schools of architecture, and among critics, it is of course universally agreed that a photograph of a building must not be confused with the building itself, but once made, the disclaimer is forgotten. Architects now retired from practice, and their dead teachers, were formed largely by buildings that they knew first and primarily from photographs. This is unfortunate, not because photographs are by nature mendacious, but because they are pictures, and therefore (by nature) not quite a satisfactory way of describing an art that is similar to sculpture. Nevertheless, the illusion of truth produced by a competent photograph has tended to fool even the architect, and it has certainly fooled the architect's client, whom the architect contradicts at his peril.

A work of architecture (a building) is hard, made of dead and rigid materials, and has in principle fixed measurements and proportions; it has façades – faces – designed to make clear where the visitor should enter, and where the photographer should stand. It is wrong, but not altogether ludicrous, to think that there might be such a thing as an objective photographic record of a work of architecture (an artefact). In any case, it is convenient to pretend that a photograph can be a surrogate for a building, so we do so, even while knowing that it is not true.

But a park is surely another matter. What critic would claim, even for tactical reasons, that a photograph (or a picture of any sort) might stand in lieu of such a place? As devil's advocate, one might nominate one of Ansel Adams's views down the valley of the Yosemite (figs. 3 and 4), but in fact Adams was able to make that picture over and over again for half a century, since the place was never twice the same.

Even the simplest of parks is more complex than Charles Garnier's Opéra. The components of a park are constantly changing size and position, or disappearing into thin air. Even in a classical French park – in which every tree is treated, one might think, as a prisoner of war, sentenced to a life of rigid obedience – even in such a place the order is mostly on the surface. Like India under the Empire, it is a site of constant insurrections, especially at the borders: incursions and migrations of native species, deaths and even plagues (to which the exotic imports are especially sensitive), struggles for light and water, Darwinian ambitions always probing and testing the gardener's defenses.

* * *

We have made no clear progress toward an answer to the question: How does one photograph a park? Perhaps the question is too difficult if asked so baldly; it might be better to think of the issue not as photographing a park, but as making photographs *in* a park. The second formulation is of course overly permissive, but if we begin (in our imaginations) by photographing everything, we can later pare away those imagined pictures that, although diverting and good to look at, seem to lie outside the intuited boundaries of our subject.

First we might eliminate all the photographs of tennis games and baseball games and other contests that do not change their nature or flavour when their own established and self-contained environments are placed within the boundaries of a park. Baseball fields, tennis courts, etc., are of course social goods, but the fact that they consume an increasingly substantial portion of our parks does not obscure the basic difference between parks and playgrounds. We might make an exception of golf, a game actually contested in a park of sorts, sometimes a park within a park. Psychologists might consider the possibility that the character of their workplace explains why the best golfers have much better manners than the best tennis players, whose working environment resembles the diagram for a Pavlovian experiment. Nevertheless, we would in the end eliminate the golfing pictures too from our imaginary portfolio, on the grounds that a golf course is a single-use park: the contest makes the place too dangerous for the poets, lovers, botanists, troubled businessmen, birdwatchers, photographers in search of themselves, and other homeless people who are the traditional clientele of twentieth-century parks as we have known (and know) them.

We would eliminate as well the pictures having to do with restaurants and art museums, and probably also the zoological gardens, that are in the parks but not really of them. Surely the great Metropolitan Museum of Art is in but not of New York's Central Park, a fact confirmed by the museum's orientation, which turns its back on the park, and by its method of expanding its domain, which is by edging backwards, like a fat man in a crowded bus.

We would with regret also exclude the stunning colour portraits of all the songbirds and waterfowl and hawks and owls that live there, not to mention the moles, voles, shrews, and mice, and the woodchucks, muskrats, and mink, even though it is a very limited park that does not have a place for them to range free. We would eliminate the pictures of the birds and beasts to avoid giving the impression that the park is for them, and that they need it, since it is in fact for us: we are the ones who need it.

Finally we would even leave out the pictures of the dog walkers and the birdwatchers and the poets and the soap-box speakers and the lovers and the would-be lovers. We would eliminate them not because they are unrepresentative or uninteresting, but because (although they are similar to us) they are not ourselves, and we enjoy our parks most deeply when we have them, or a small corner in one of them, to ourselves.

The photographers whose work is gathered here have given us different places than those that Olmsted made, but their aim was in a sense perhaps similar to his; both he and they have given us places that we complete by entering into them – in the first case physically, and in the second imaginatively.

* * *

From our imaginary portfolio we seem to have eliminated everything except pictures of the place itself – whatever we might mean by that. It is easy to locate a park on a map, but not easy to define or even describe its nature, beyond saying that it is in the growing season predominantly green. Is it a pattern of roads and footpaths and other architectural artefacts, or a community of plants, or a geological stage on which unfolds a long, slow, plotless drama? Is it a collection of three-dimensional echoes of great moments in landscape painting – nature's own *tableaux vivants*? Let us grant that it is all of these things and more, and ask whether any of them can be satisfactorily photographed. The answer must be, not exactly. What the photographer tries to do instead is make a good photograph (a thing in harmony with the logic of its own processes), which also describes a particular aspect or detail of the large subject, and which sometimes, with luck, will be consonant in its own rhythms and structure with the photographer's intuition of the nature of the place.

Critics who are not photographers often divide photography into two camps: one is called documentary, suggesting that it has a privileged access to the truth, and the other is called creative, or personal, or expressive, suggesting that it has a privileged access to art. The best photographers generally shun this dichotomy, understanding that it does a disservice to both truth and art, and also to the integrity of photography, which – regardless of camps – is a method of describing how things look.

The parks described here have looked very different to the three photographers who have studied them. We might say that Robert Burley sees the parks as artefacts, that Geoffrey James sees them as ancient farms in decline, and that Lee Friedlander sees them as jungles dreaming of civilization. But however we would describe the differences between their views, it would be wrong, I think, to ascribe them to conscious intention, and more wrong still to ascribe the differences to the pursuit of style – to the search for an individual (personal, unique, marketable) way of seeing. I believe that each of them did the same thing: they tried, within the limits of their own artistic histories, talents, and technical commitments, to make photographs – little pictures on paper – that would describe how the place looked.

PORTFOLIO

GEOFFREY JAMES

ROBERT BURLEY

LEE FRIEDLANDER

GEOFFREY JAMES

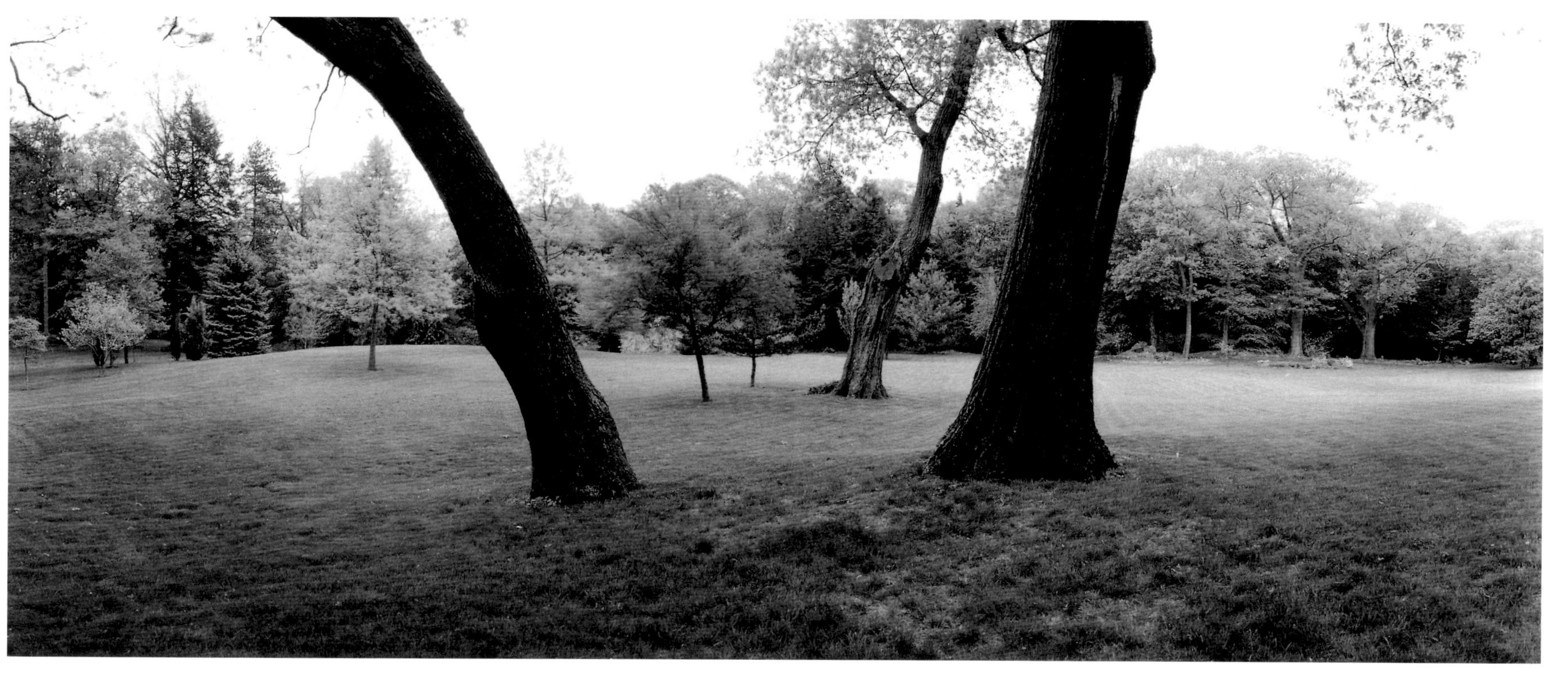

SOUTHWOOD, 1993

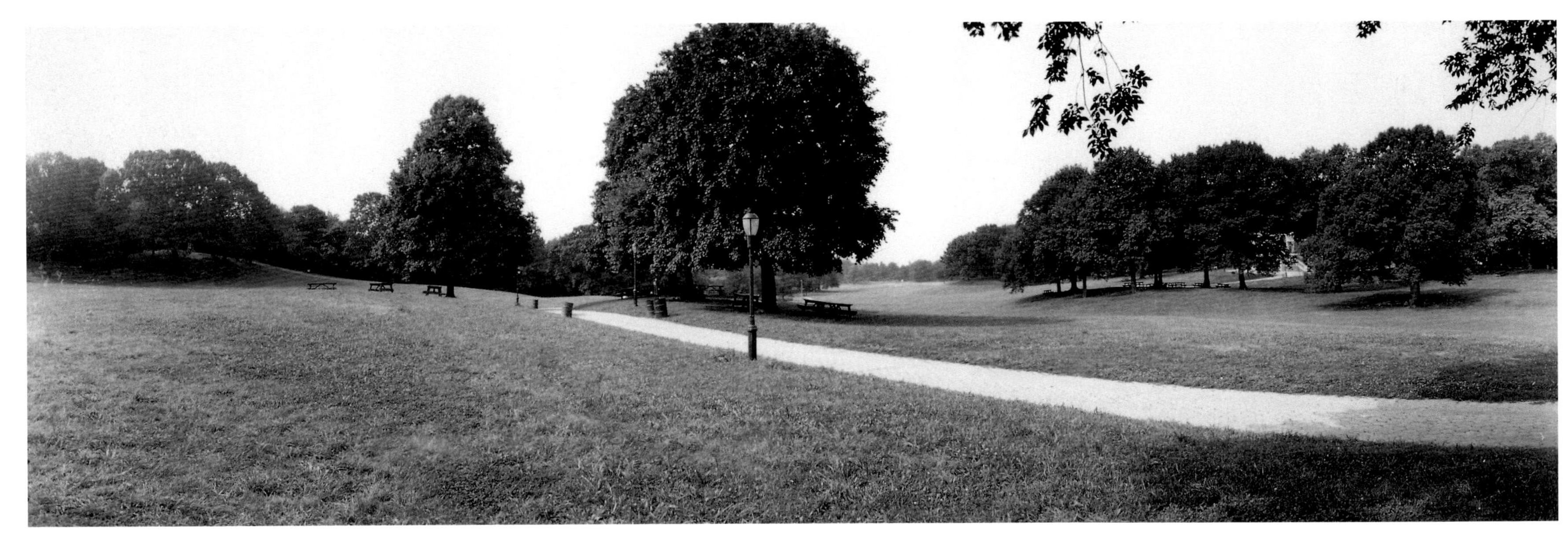

PROSPECT PARK, 1989

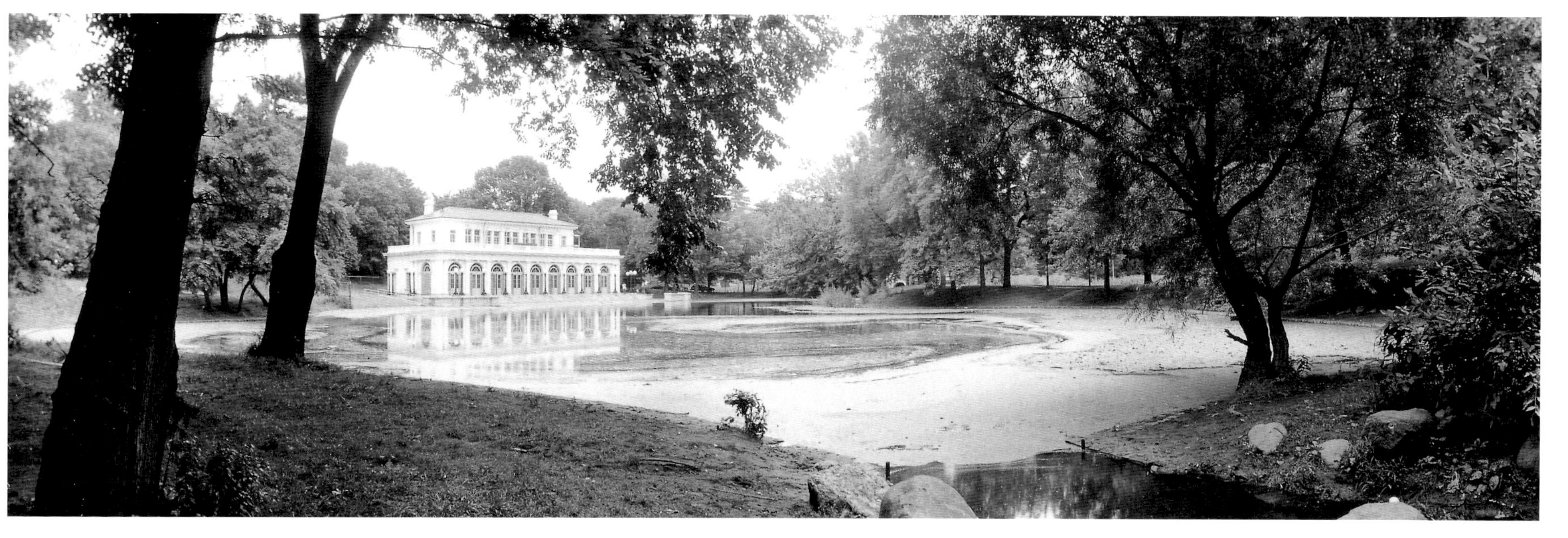

PROSPECT PARK, 1989

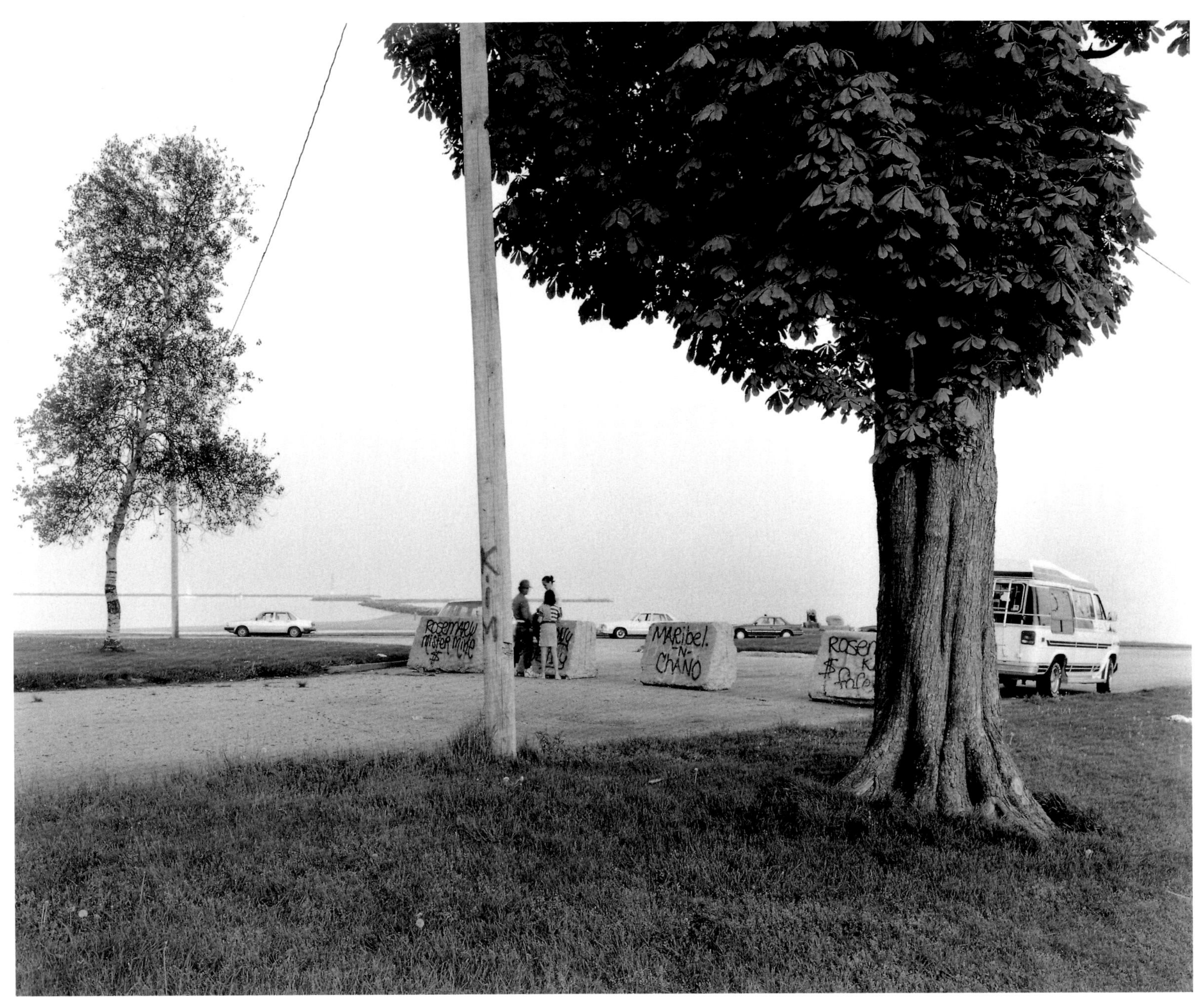

SEASIDE PARK, 1991

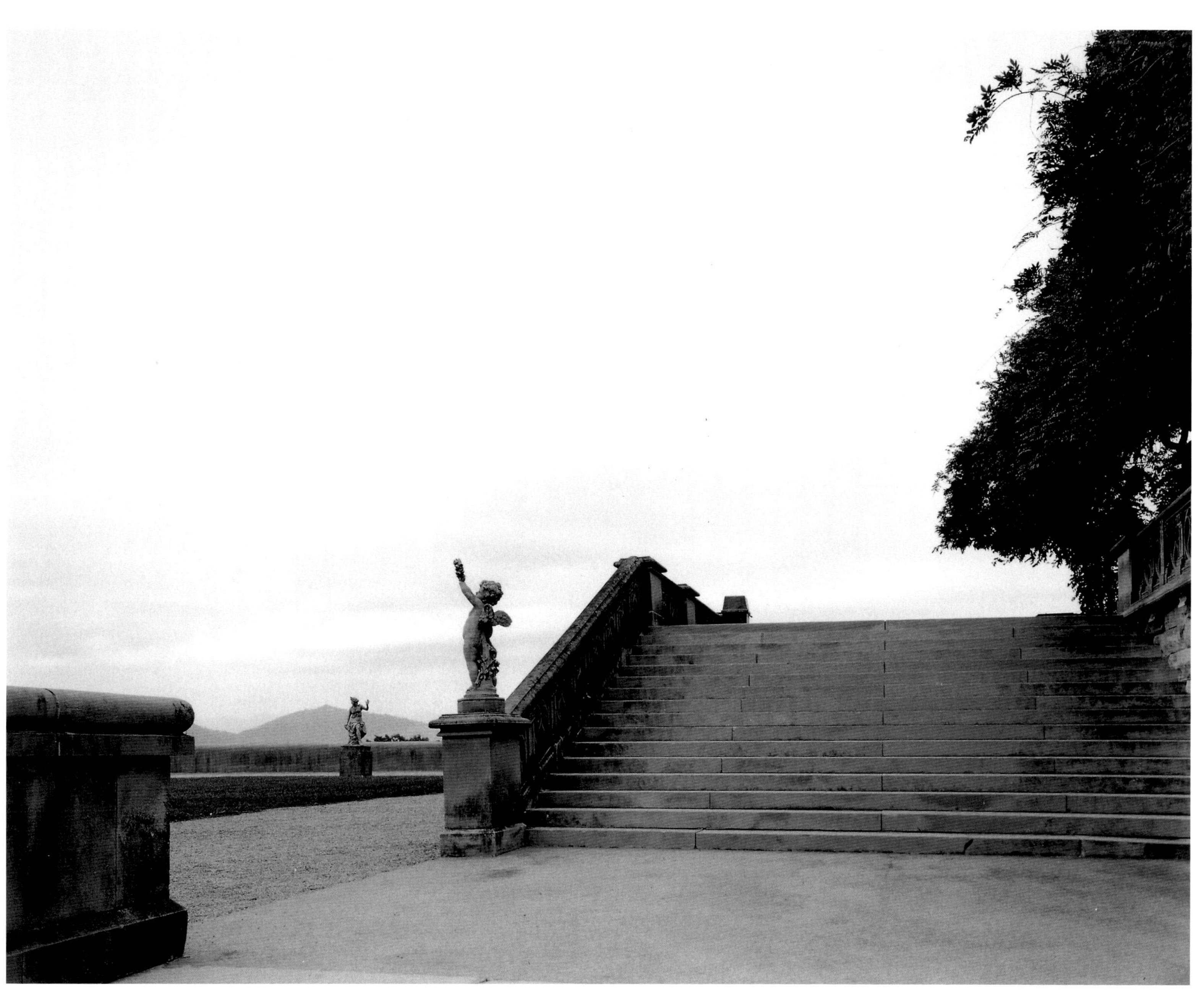

BILTMORE, 1990

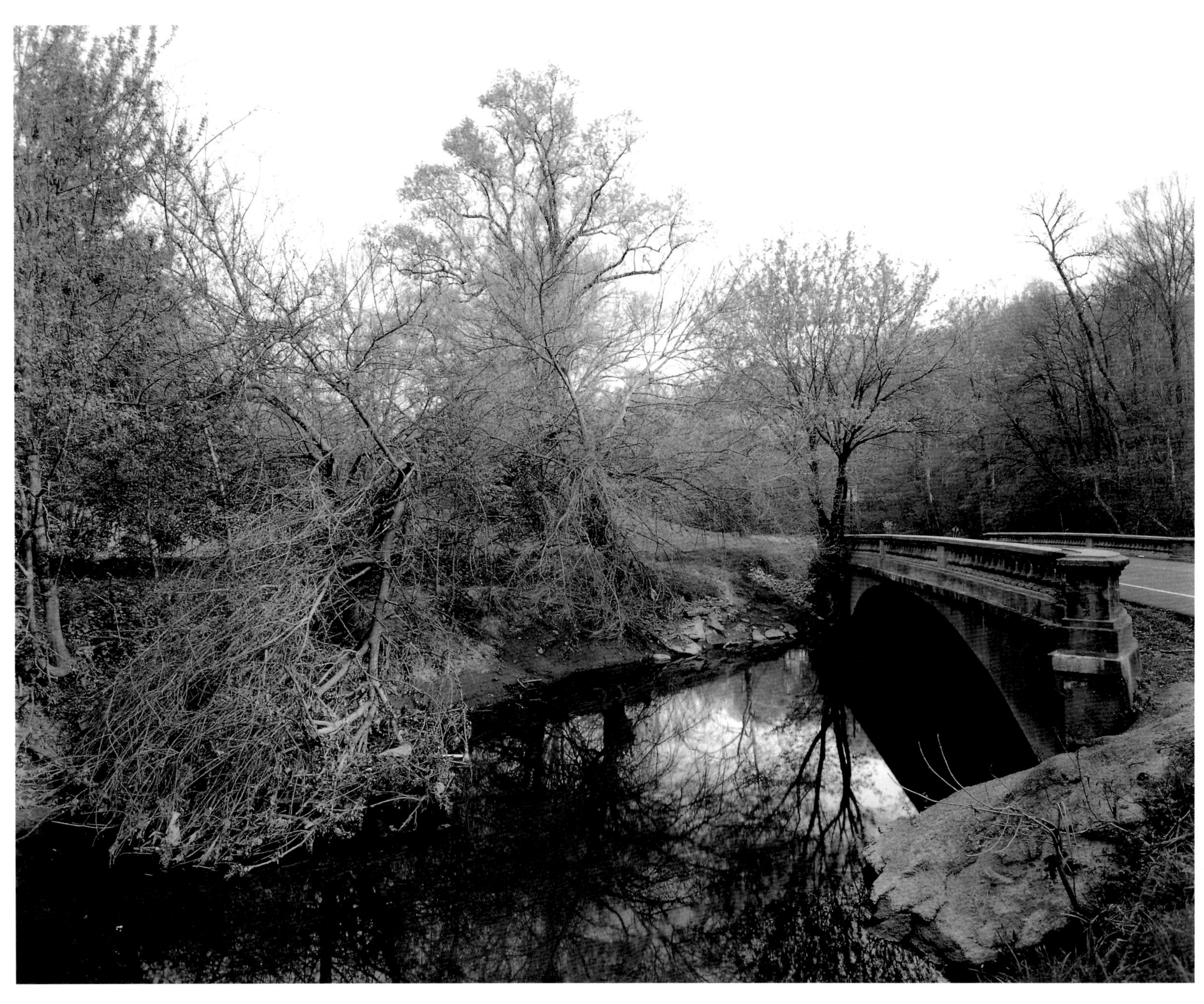

CHEROKEE PARK, 1993

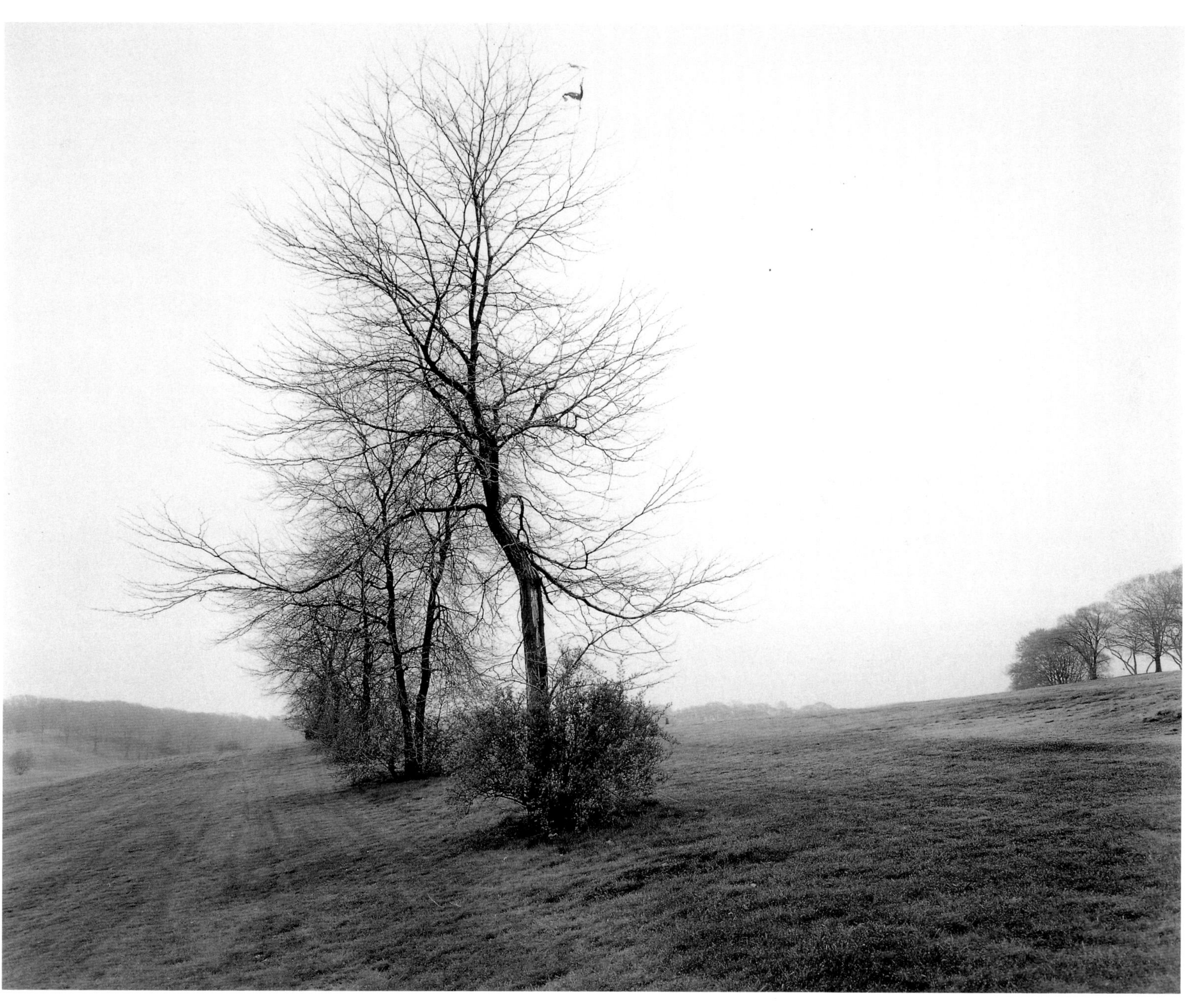

FRANKLIN PARK, 1991

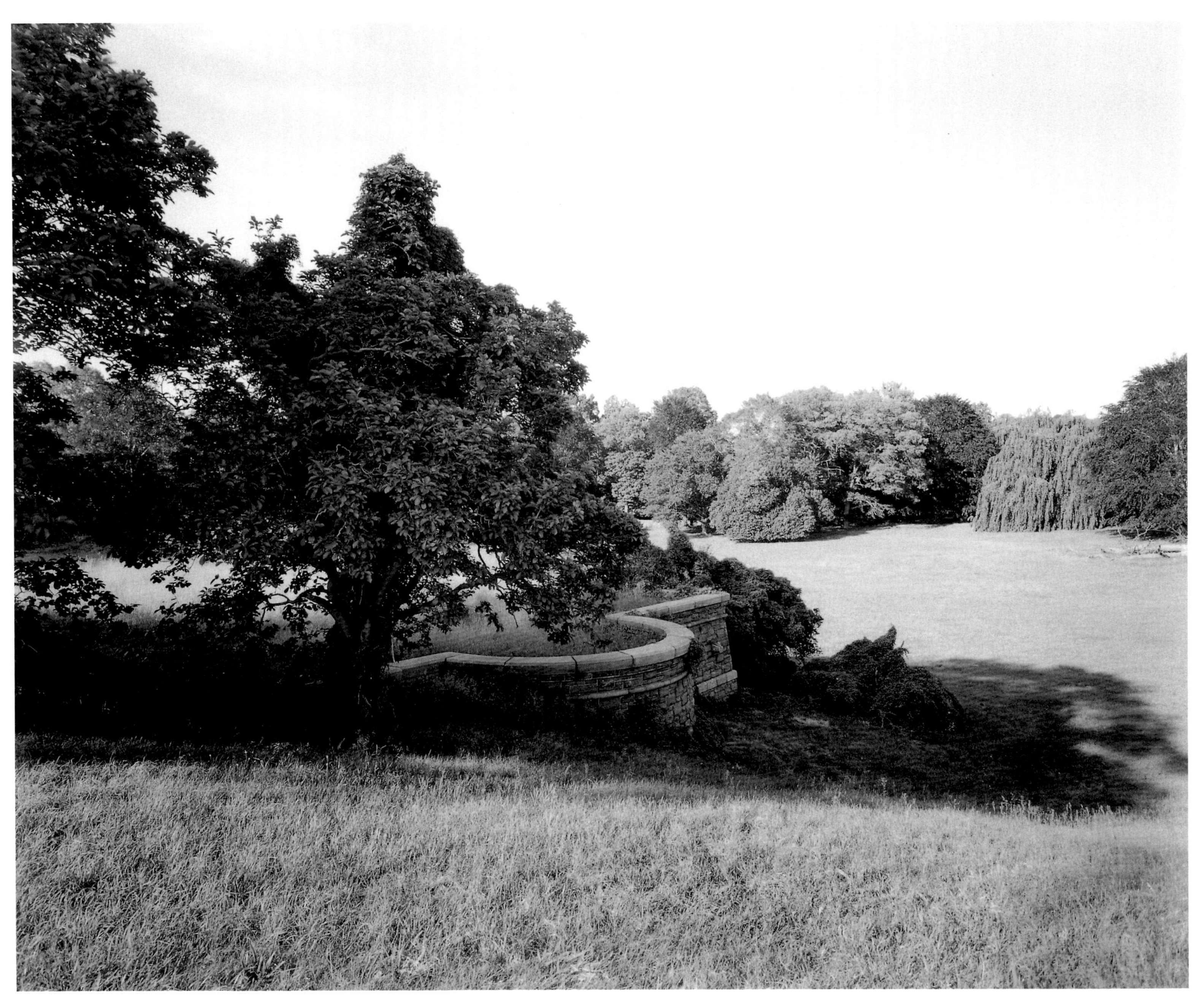

ROCKWOOD HALL, 1994

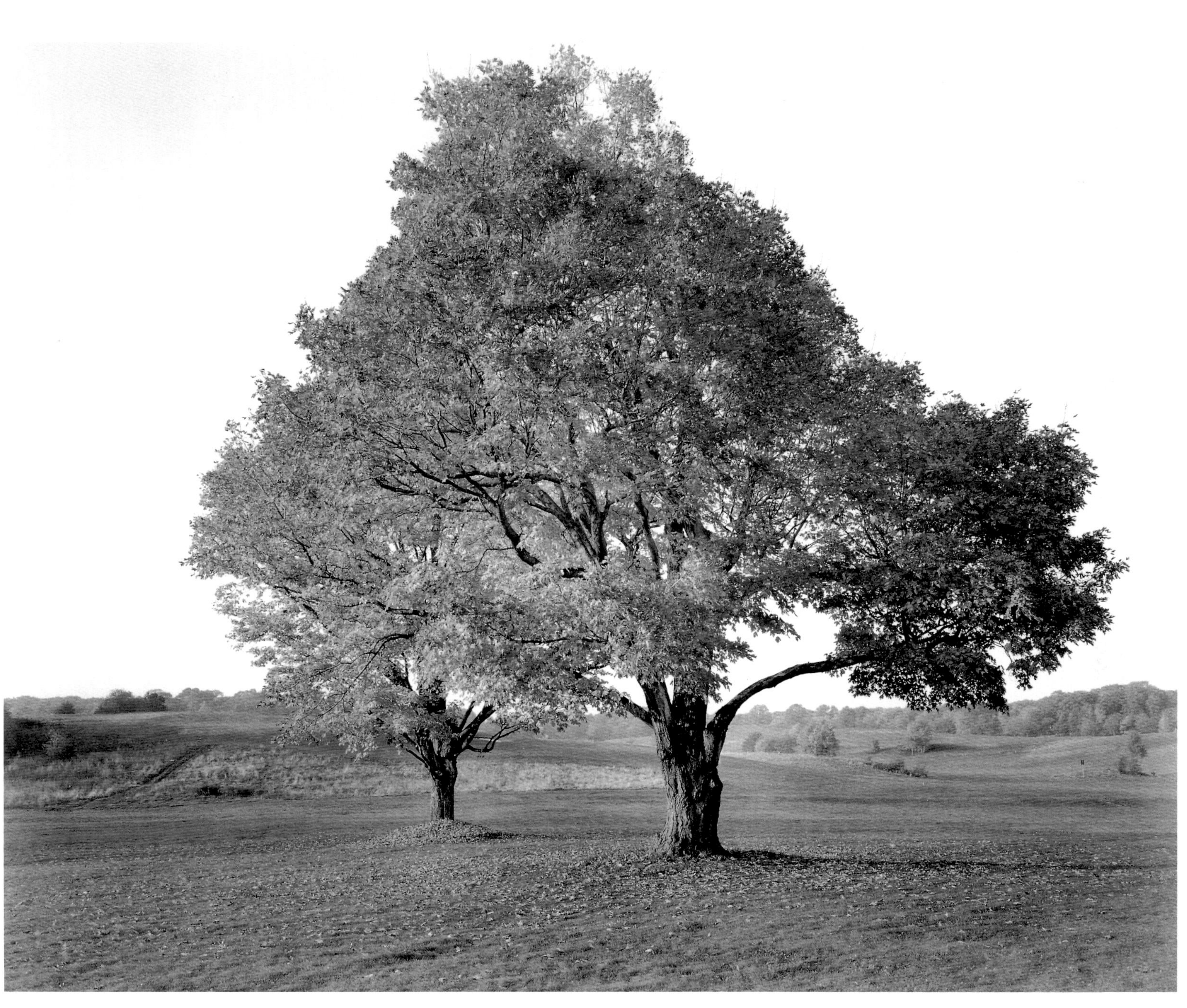

FRANKLIN PARK, 1991

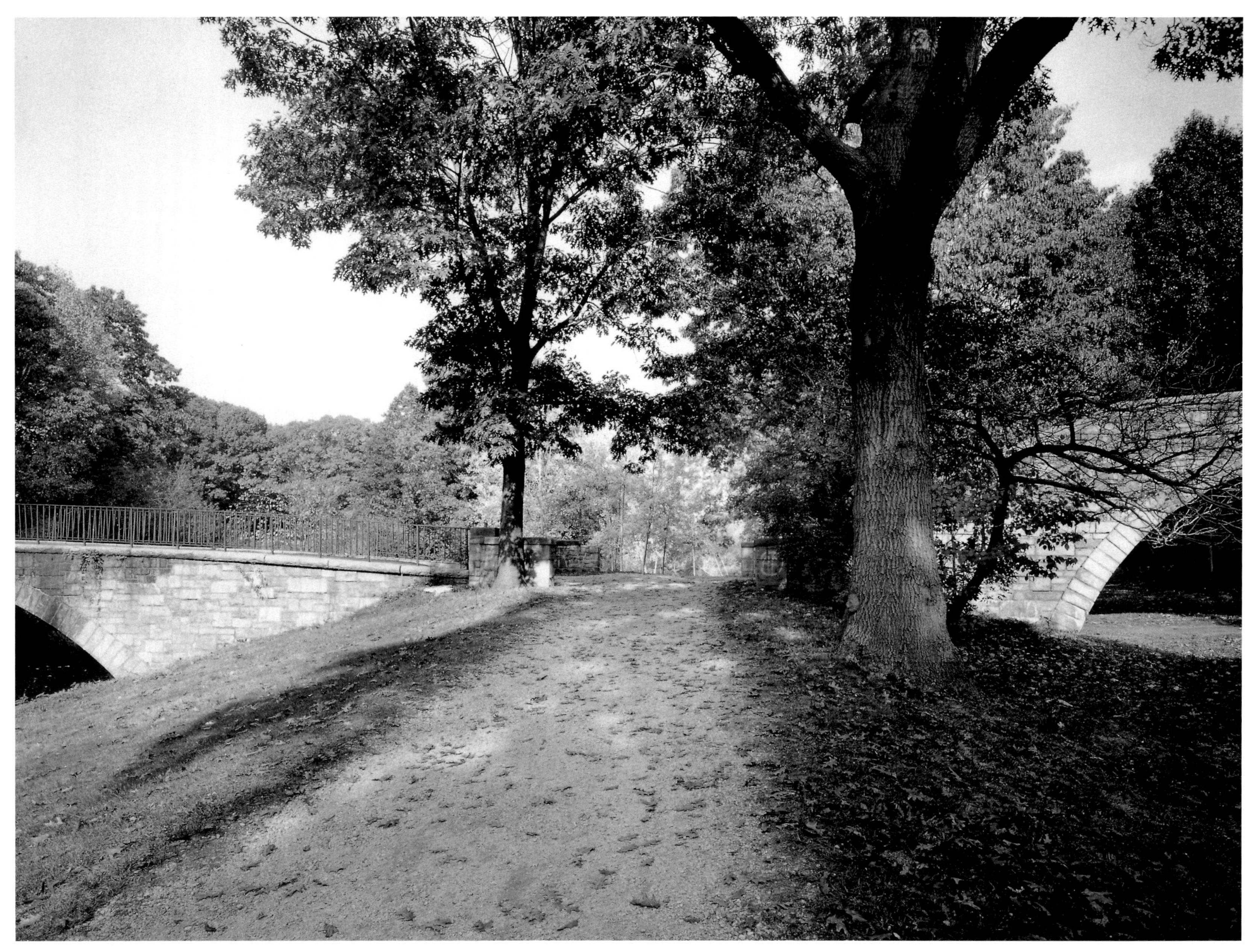

THE MUDDY RIVER IMPROVEMENT, 1991

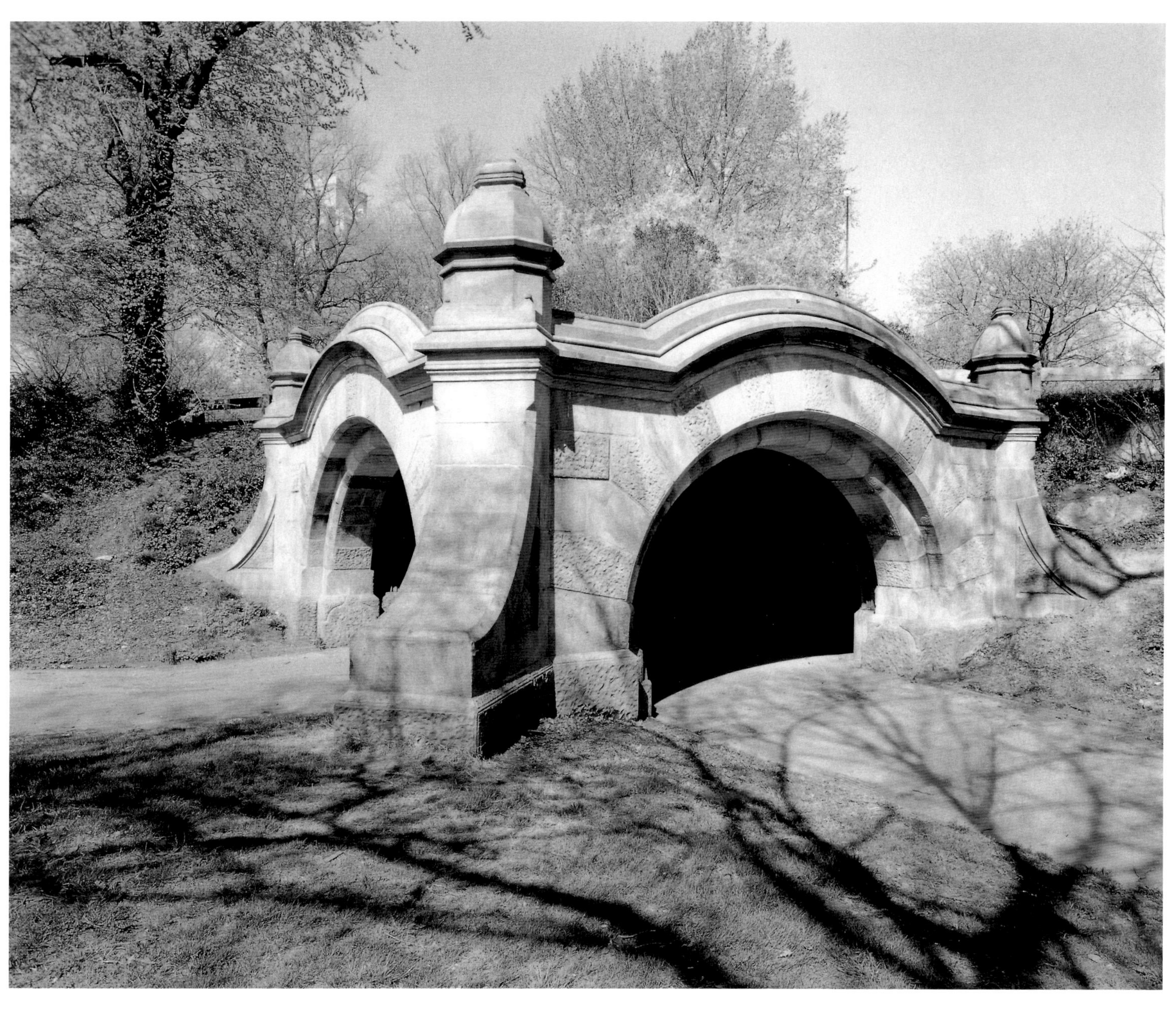

PROSPECT PARK, 1994

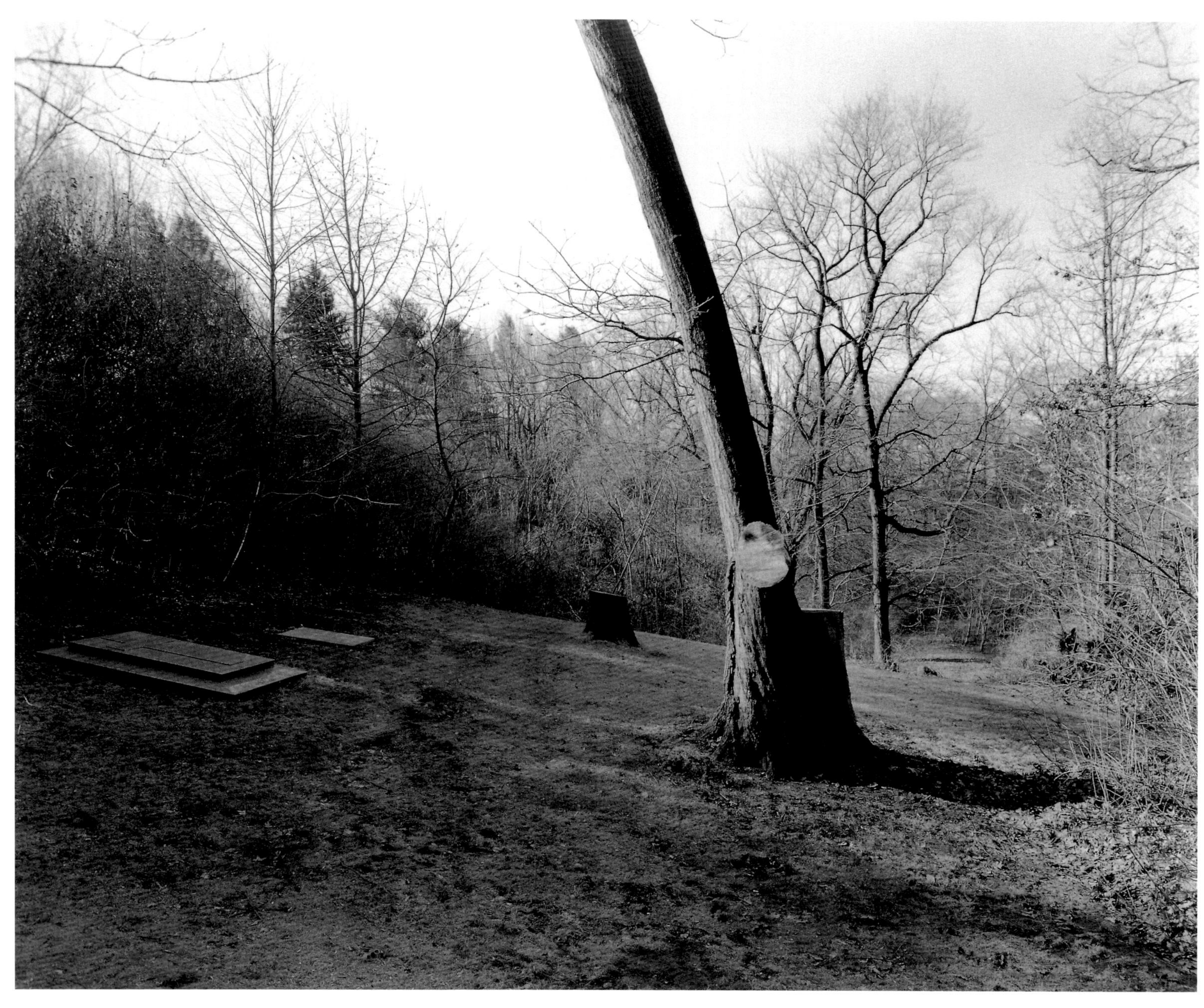

THE VANDERBILT CEMETERY, 1993

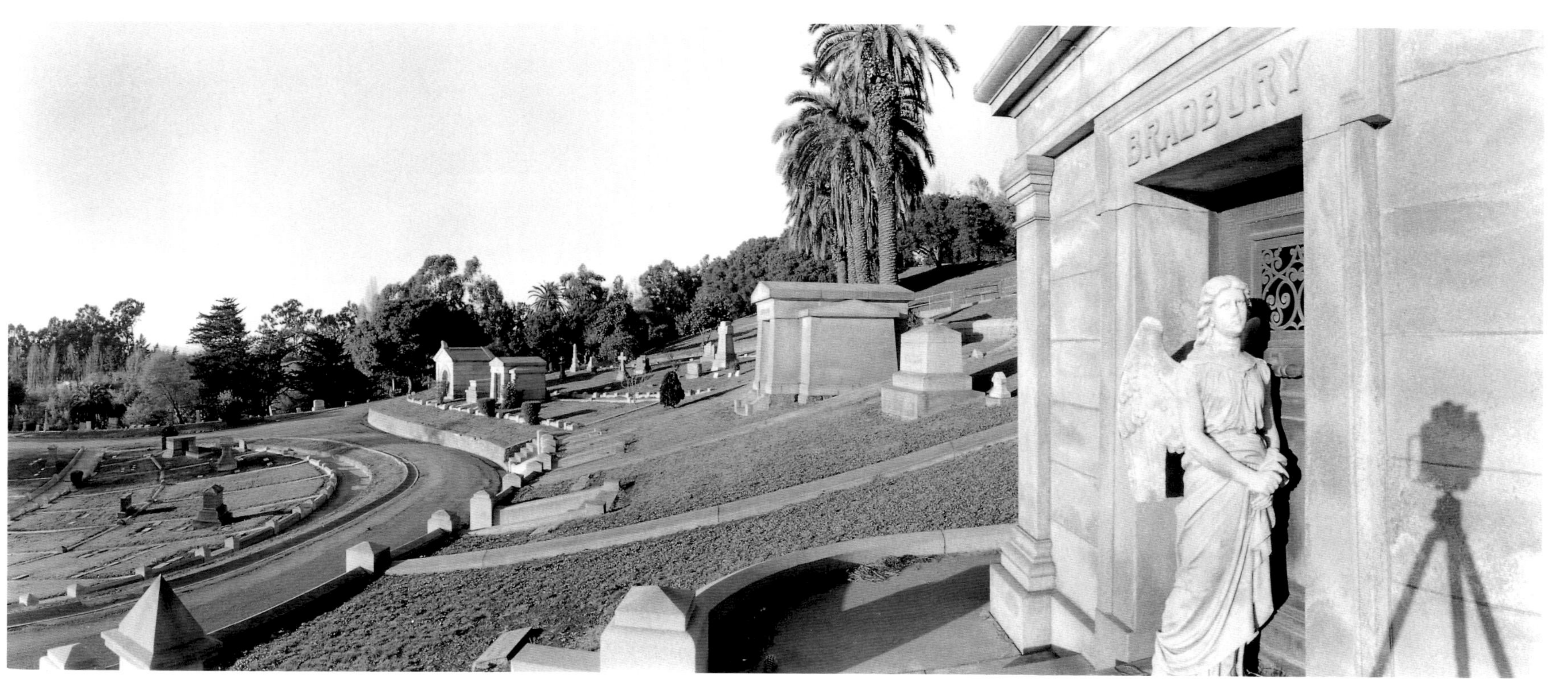

MOUNTAIN VIEW CEMETERY, 1993

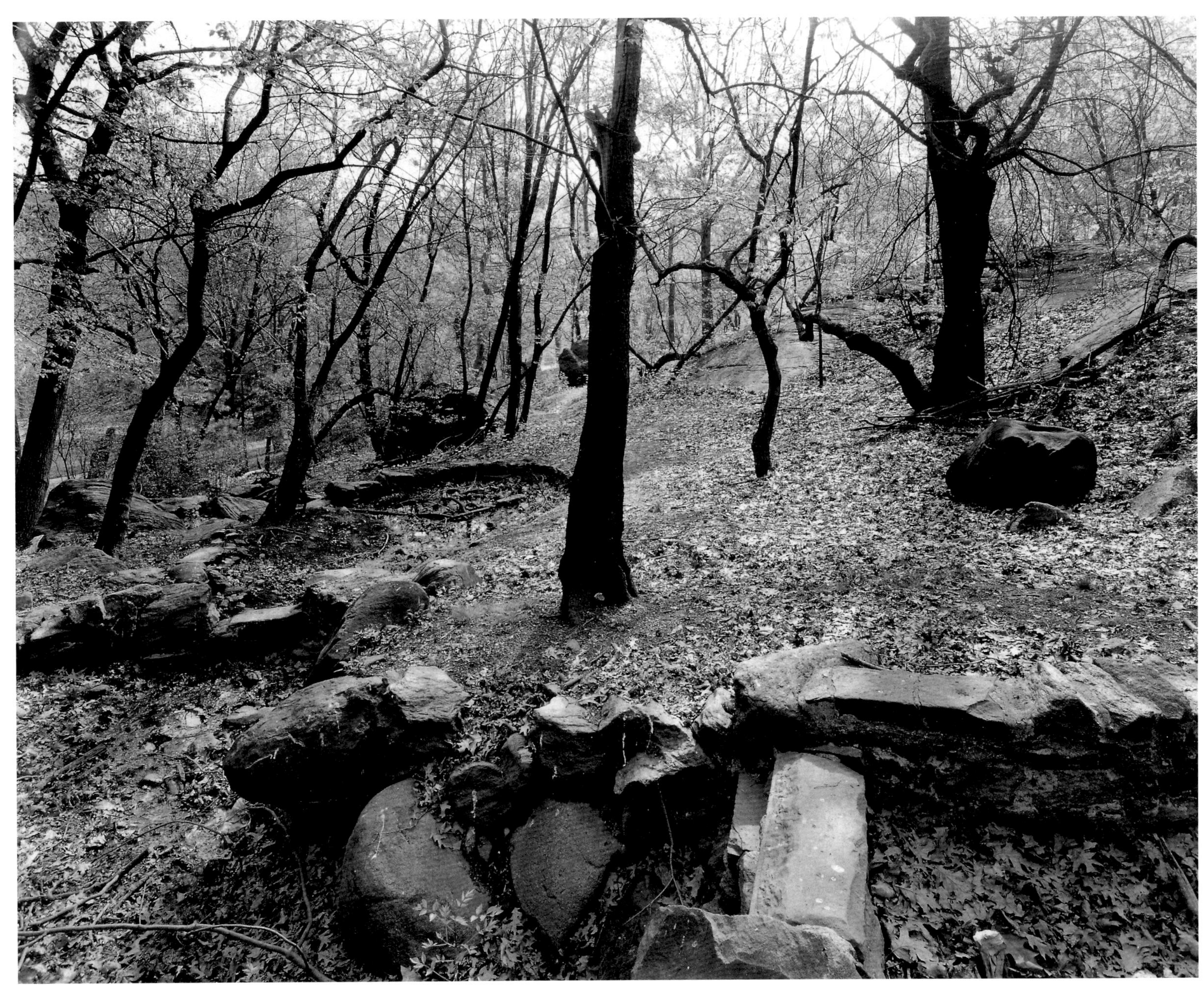

CENTRAL PARK, 1994

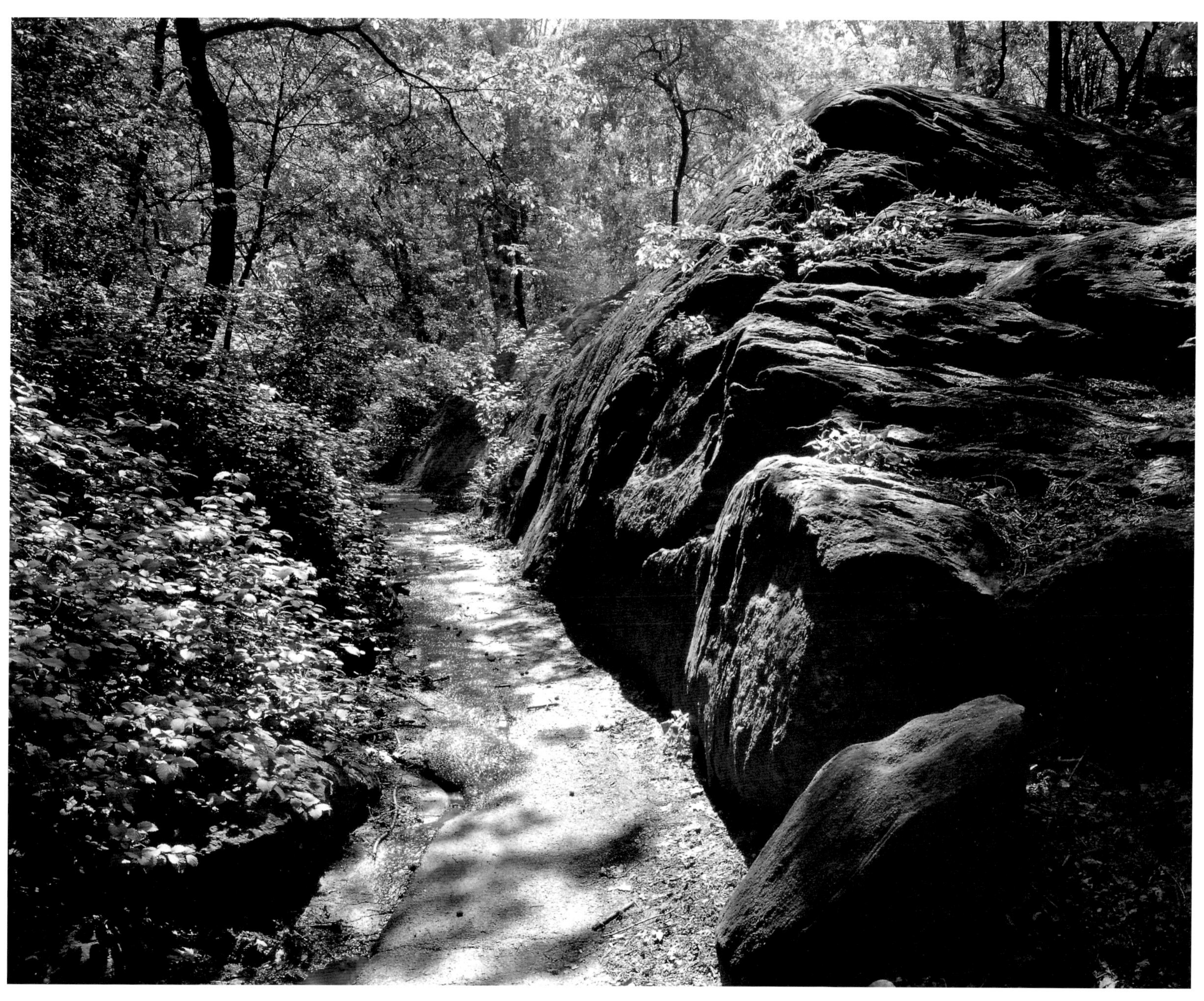

CENTRAL PARK, 1992

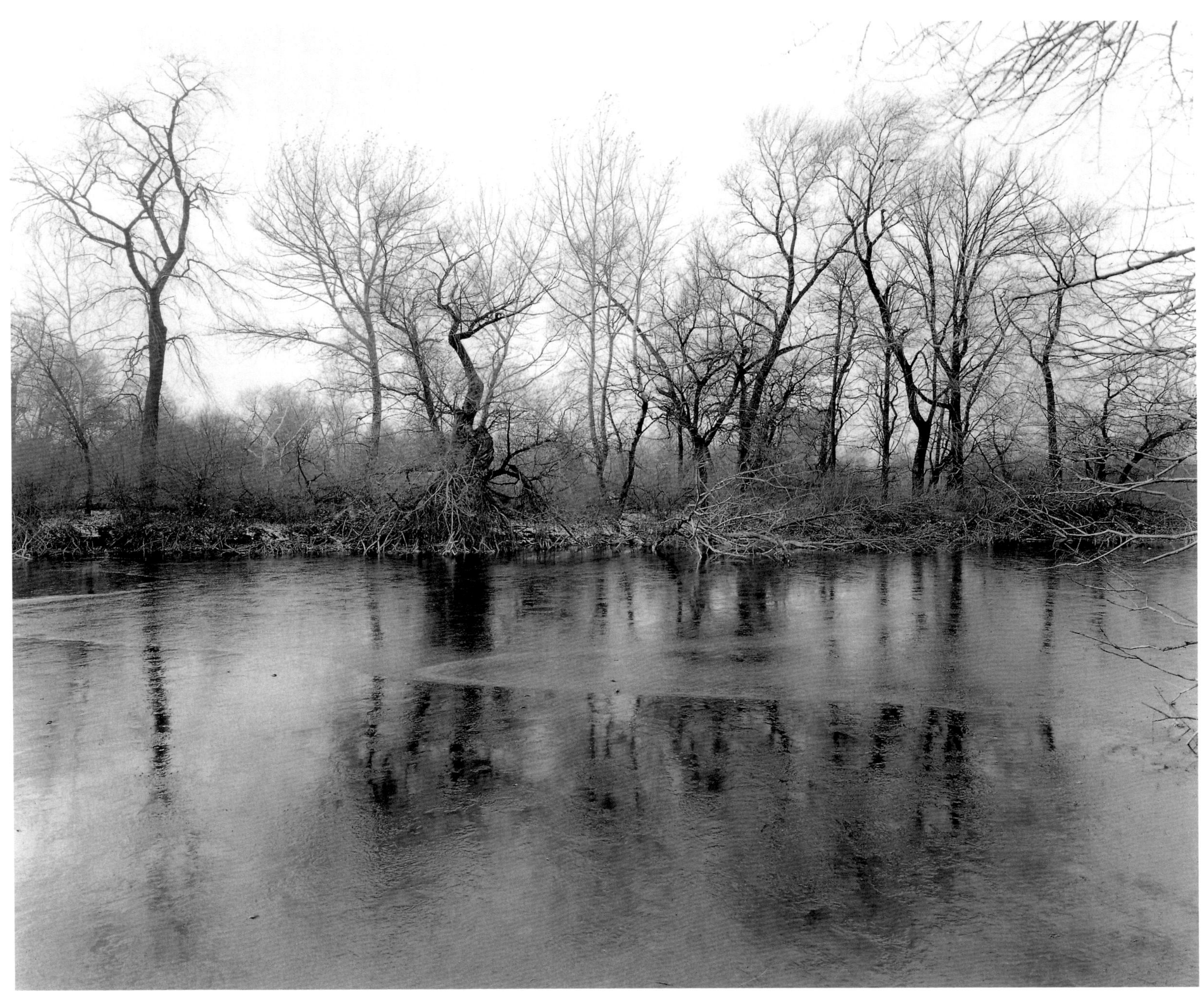

JACKSON PARK, 1991

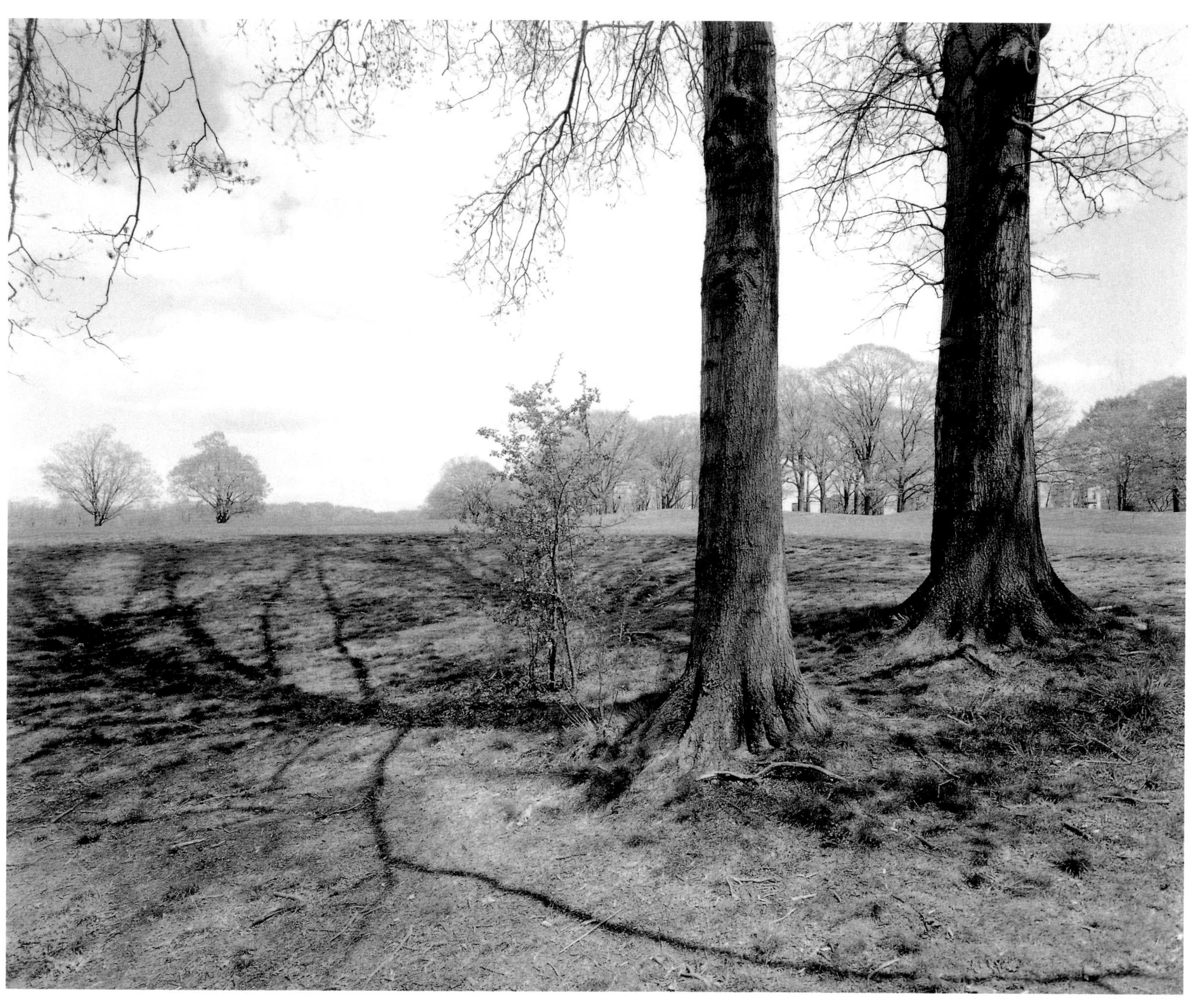

FRANKLIN PARK, 1994

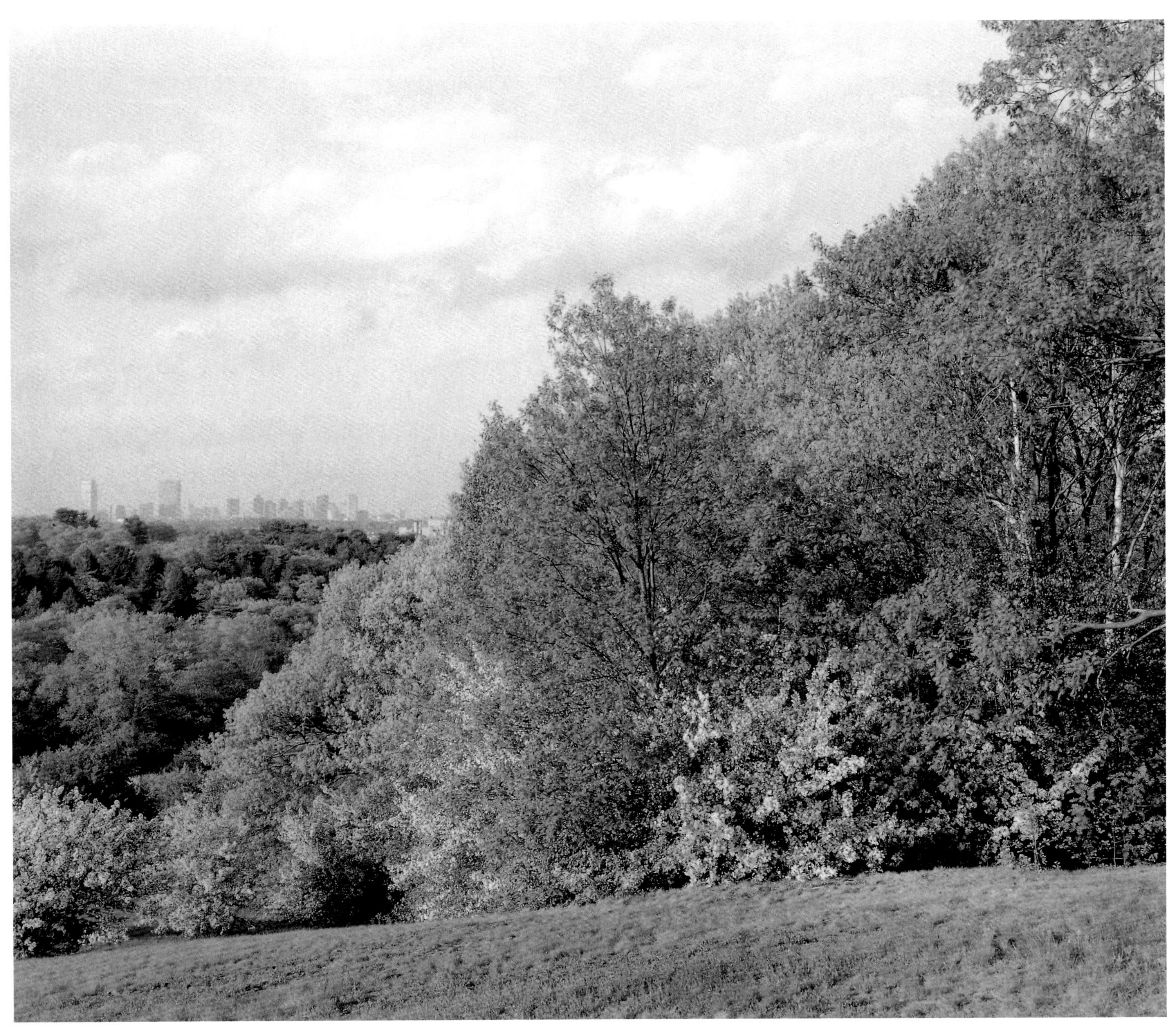

ARNOLD ARBORETUM, 1993

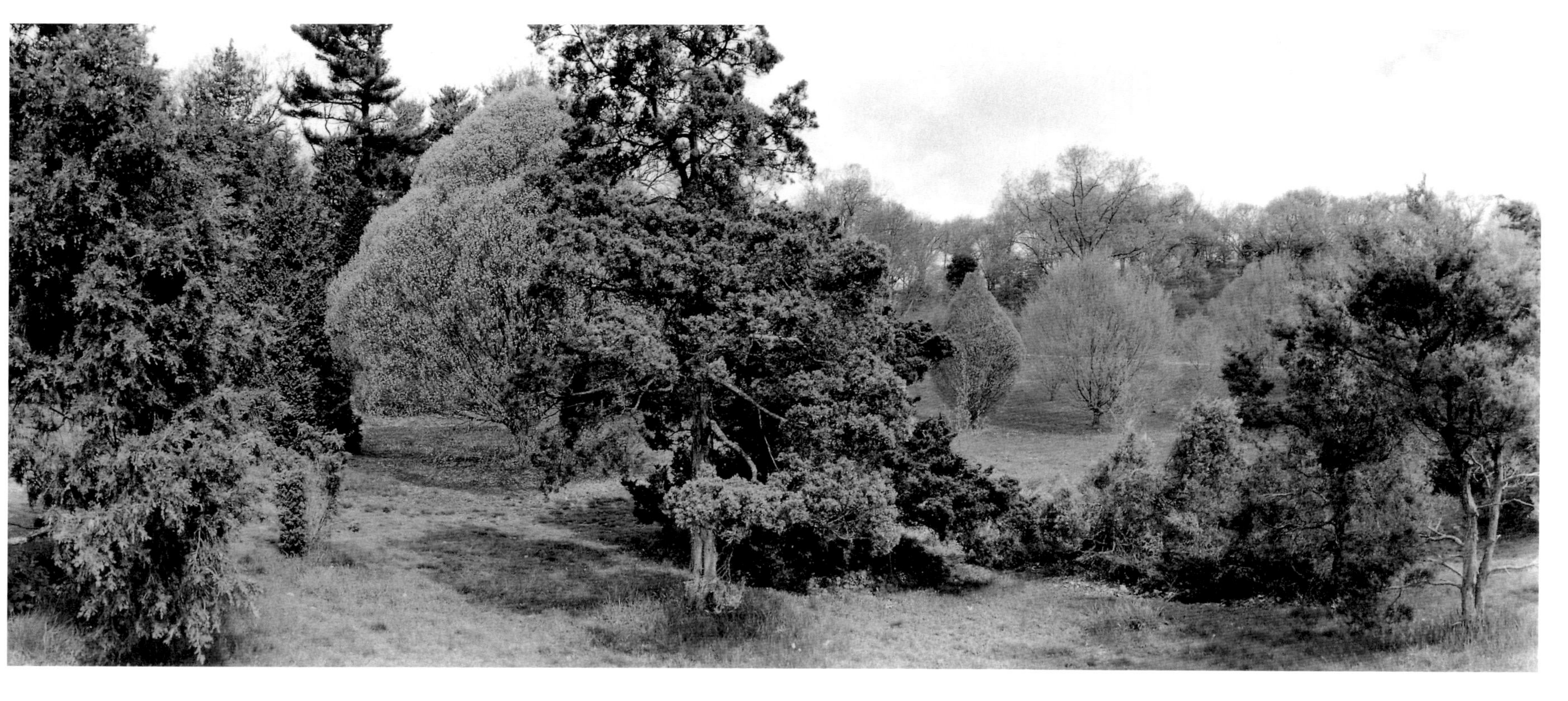

ARNOLD ARBORETUM, 1994

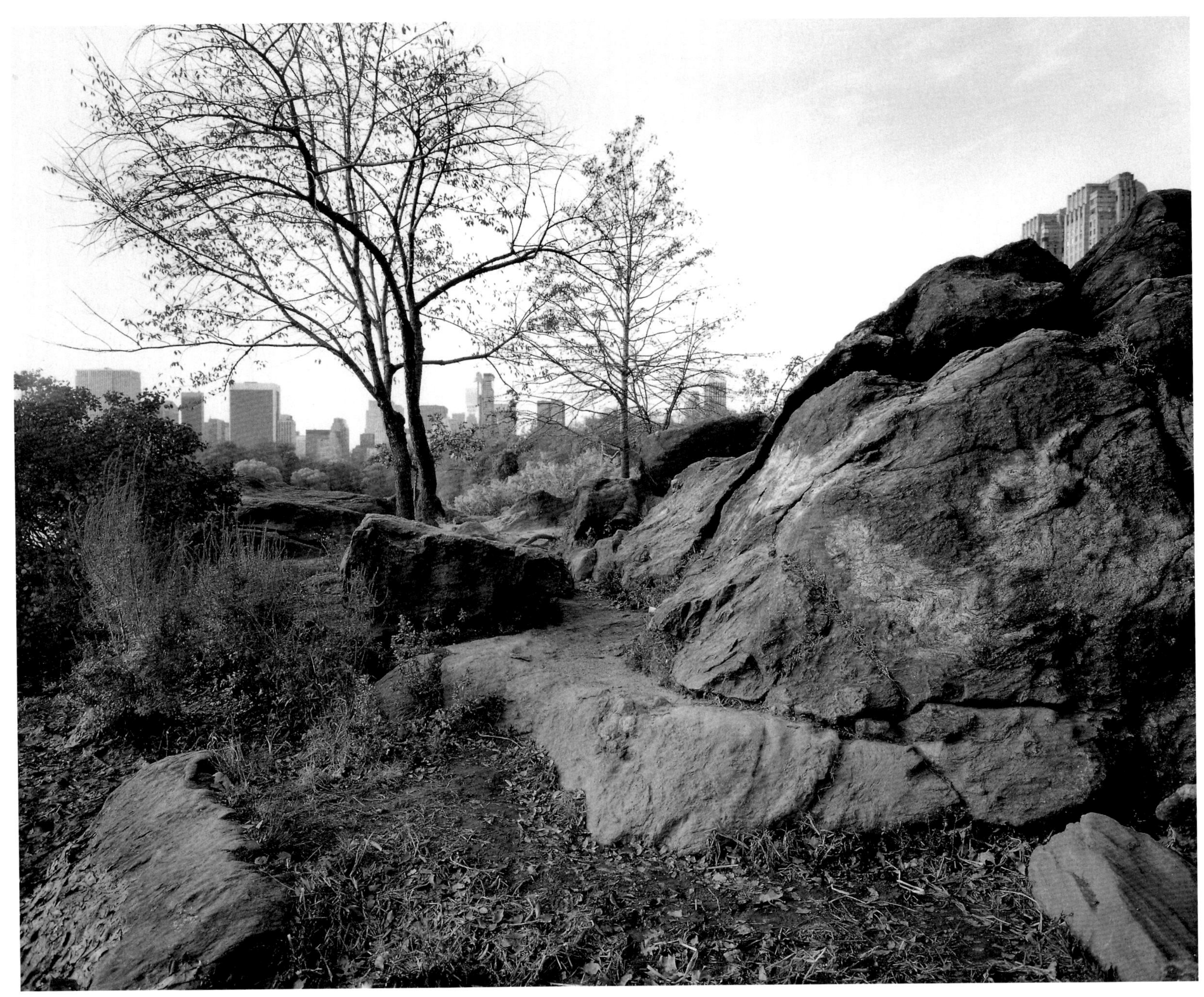

CENTRAL PARK, 1991

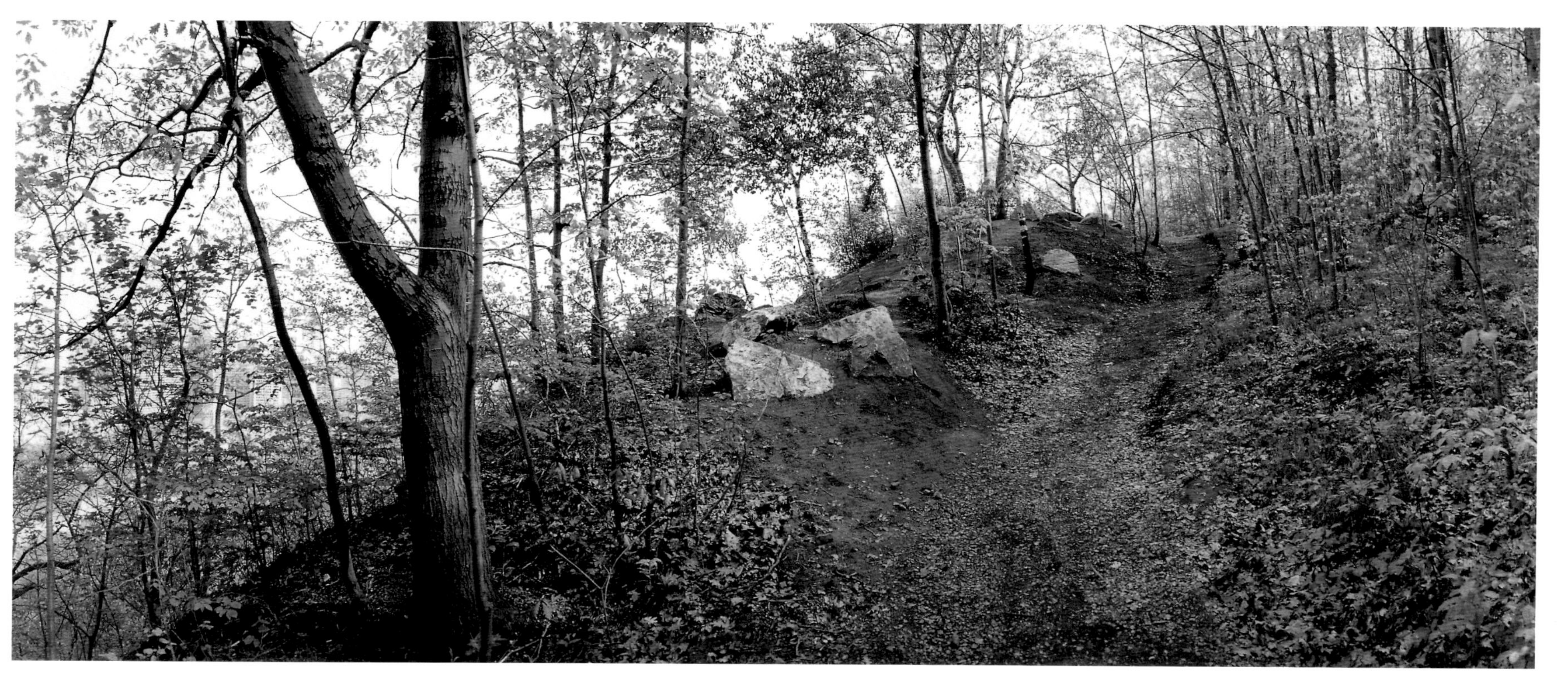

PARC DU MONT-ROYAL, 1994

ROBERT BURLEY

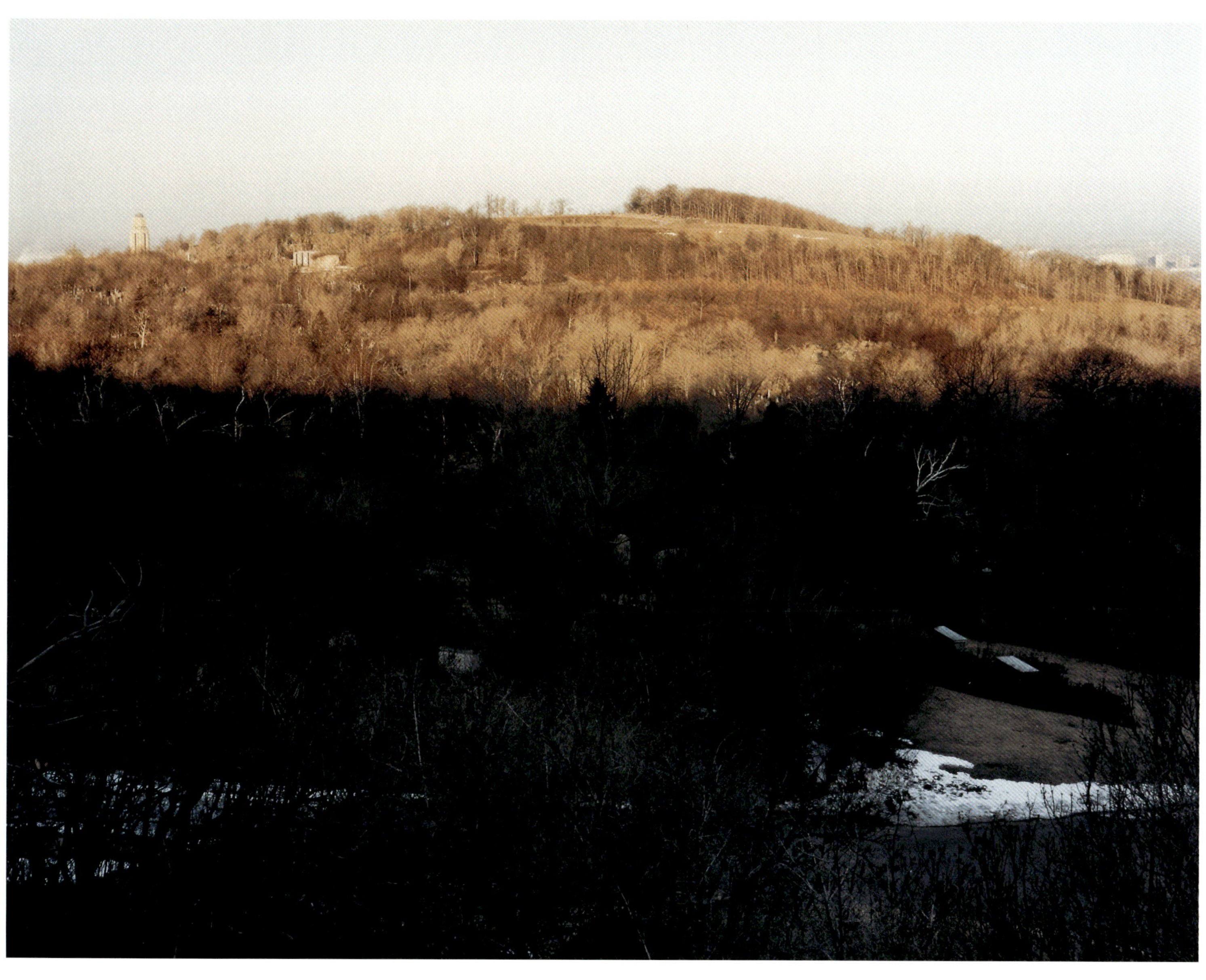

PARC DU MONT-ROYAL, 1990

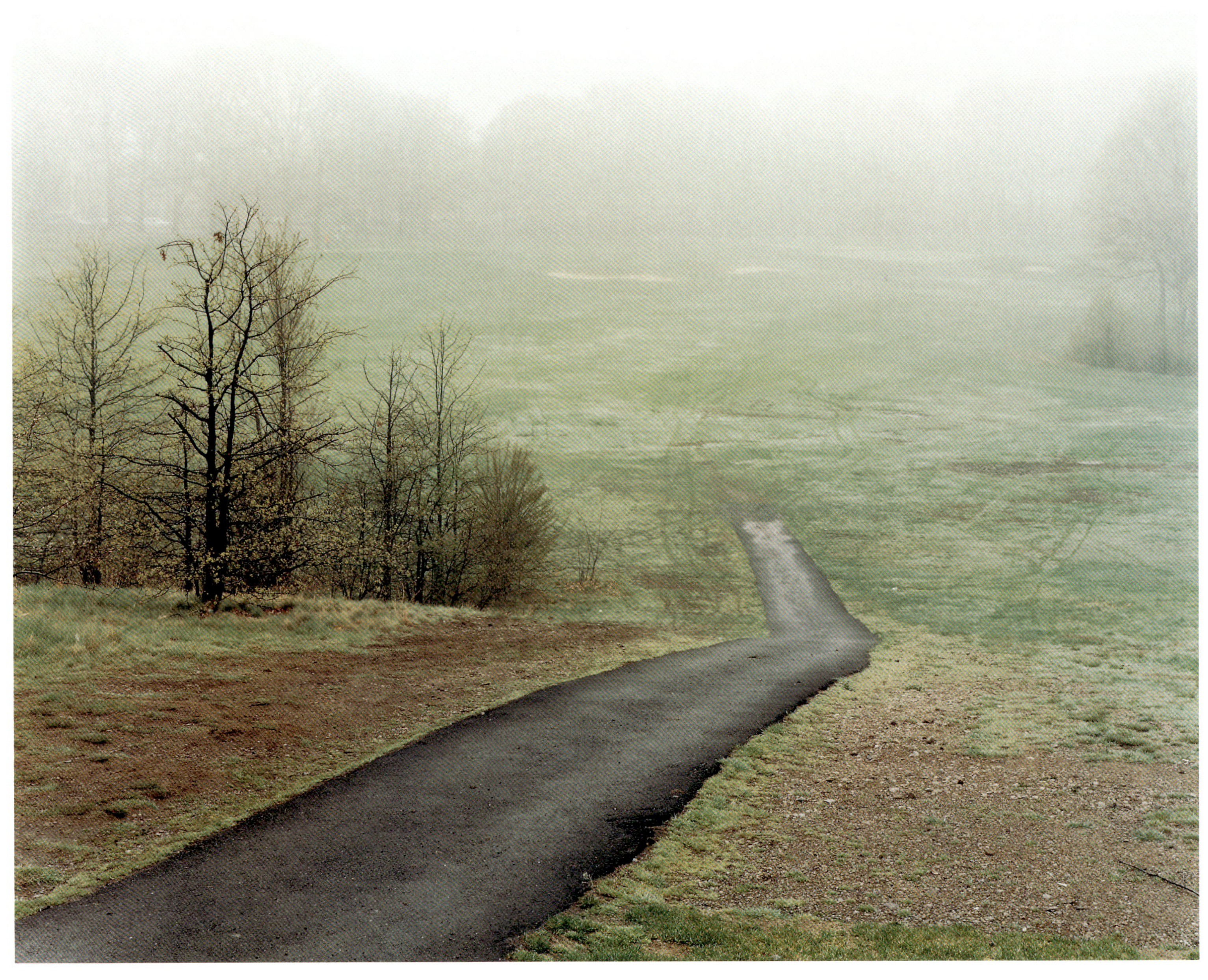

FRANKLIN PARK, 1994

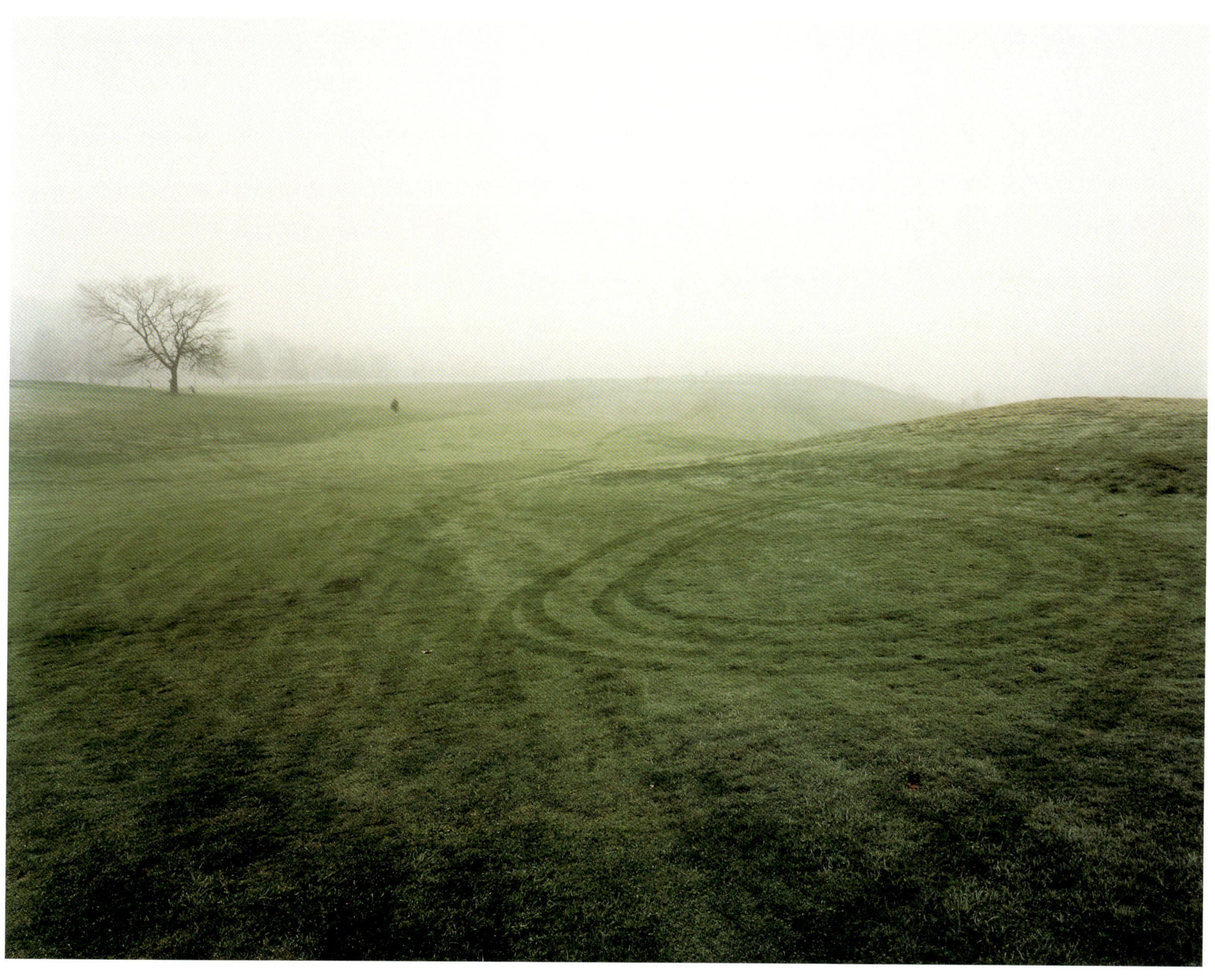

FRANKLIN PARK, 1994

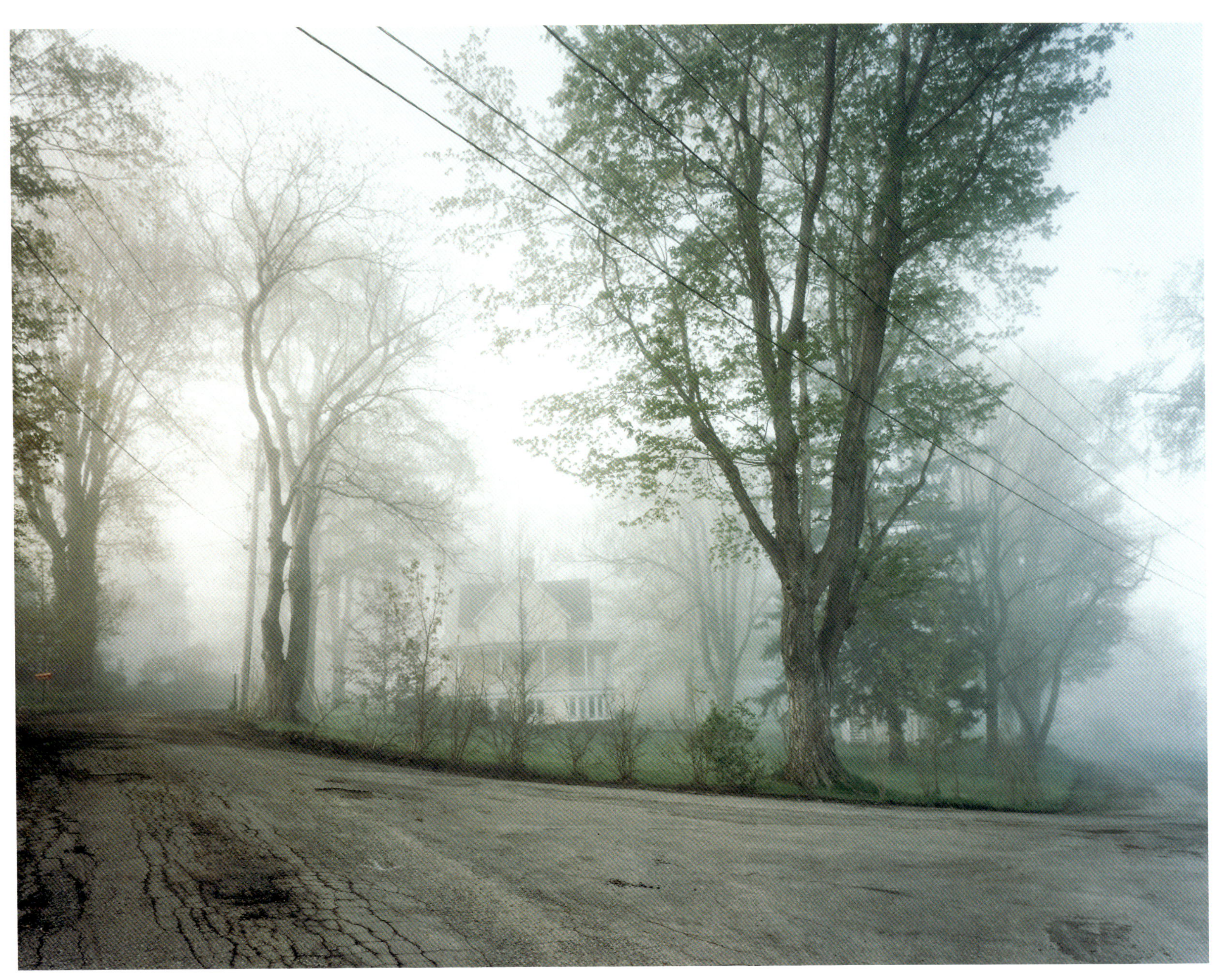

POINT CHAUTAUQUA, 1994

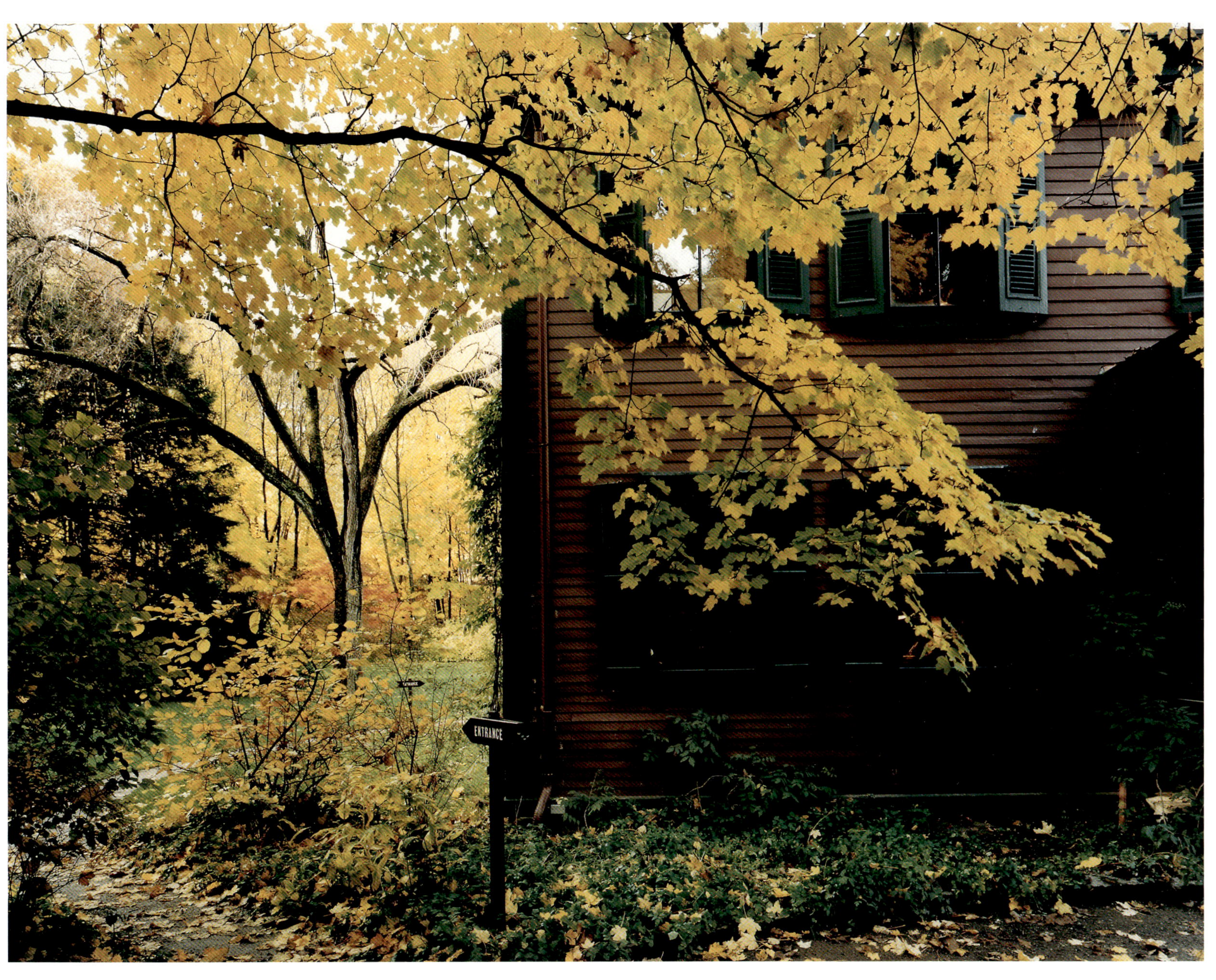

FAIRSTED, 1992

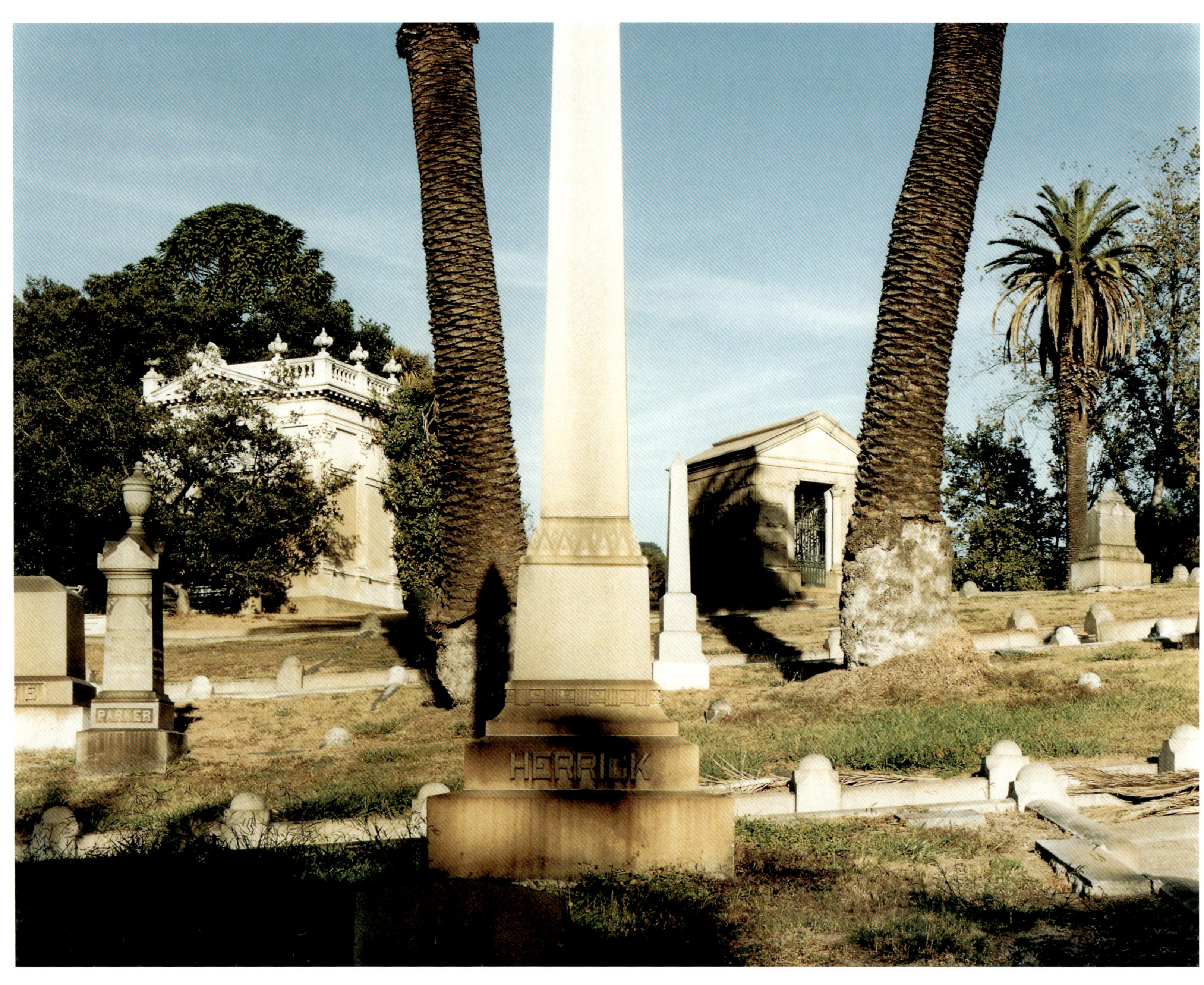

MOUNTAIN VIEW CEMETERY, 1991

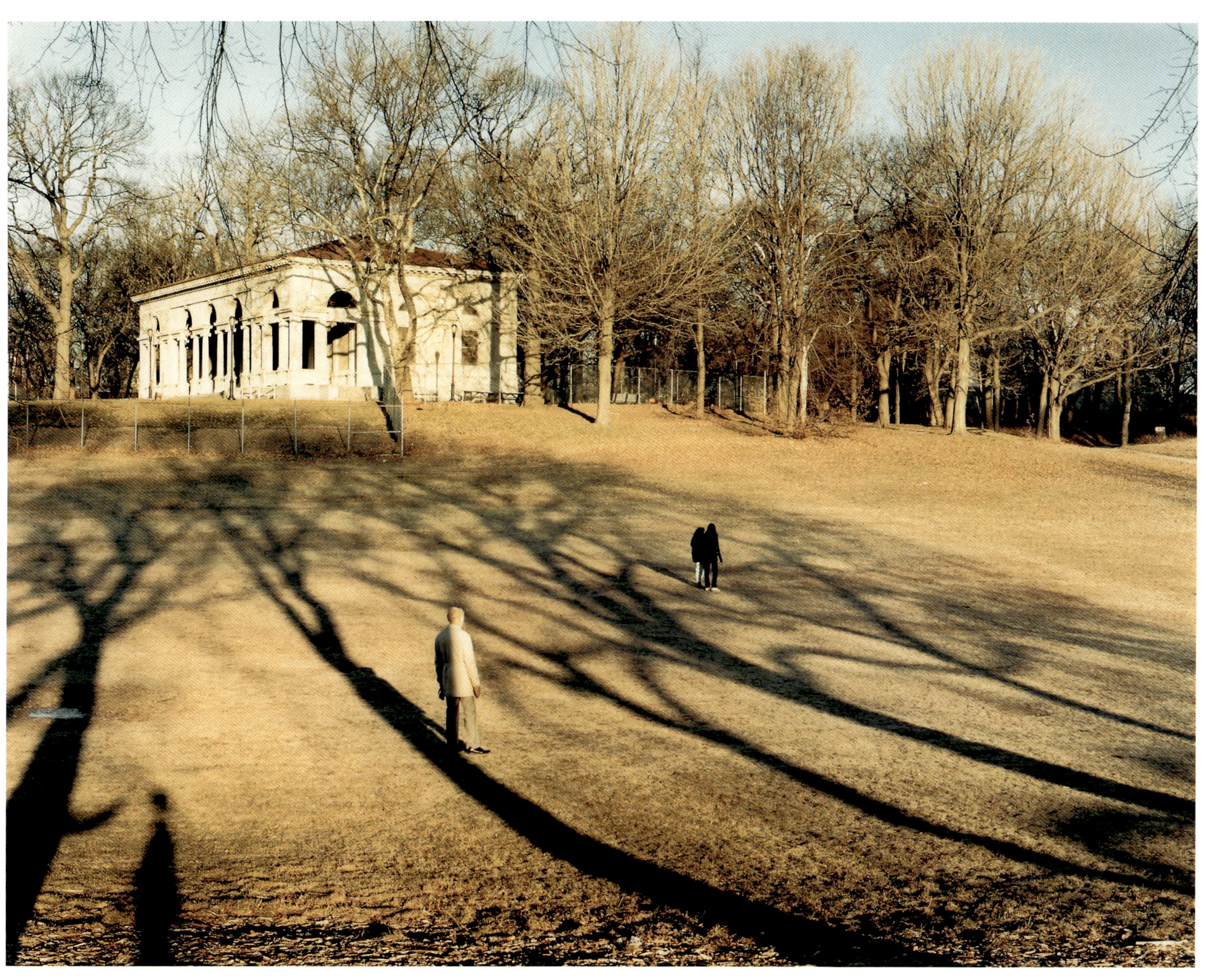

PROSPECT PARK, 1990

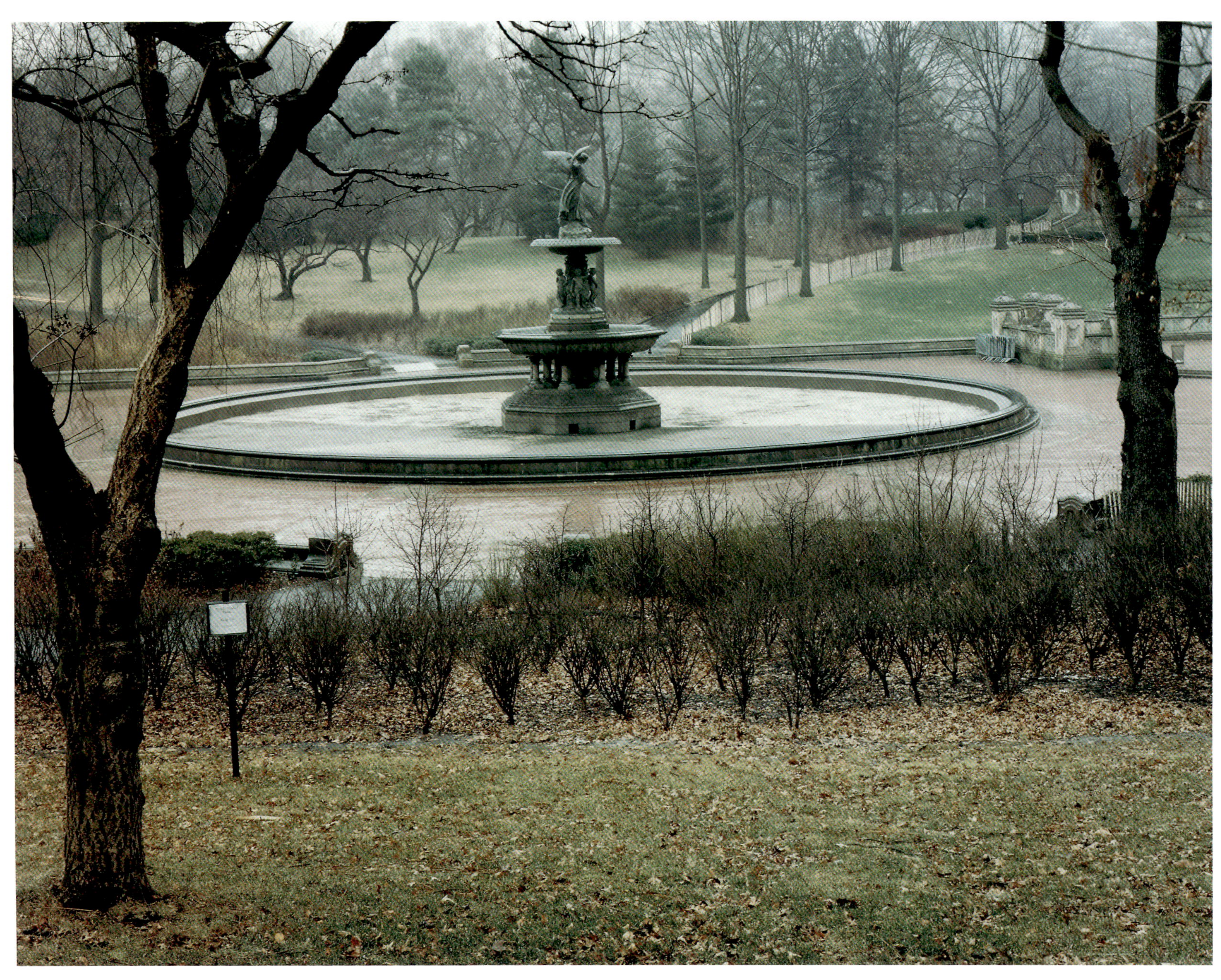

CENTRAL PARK, 1990

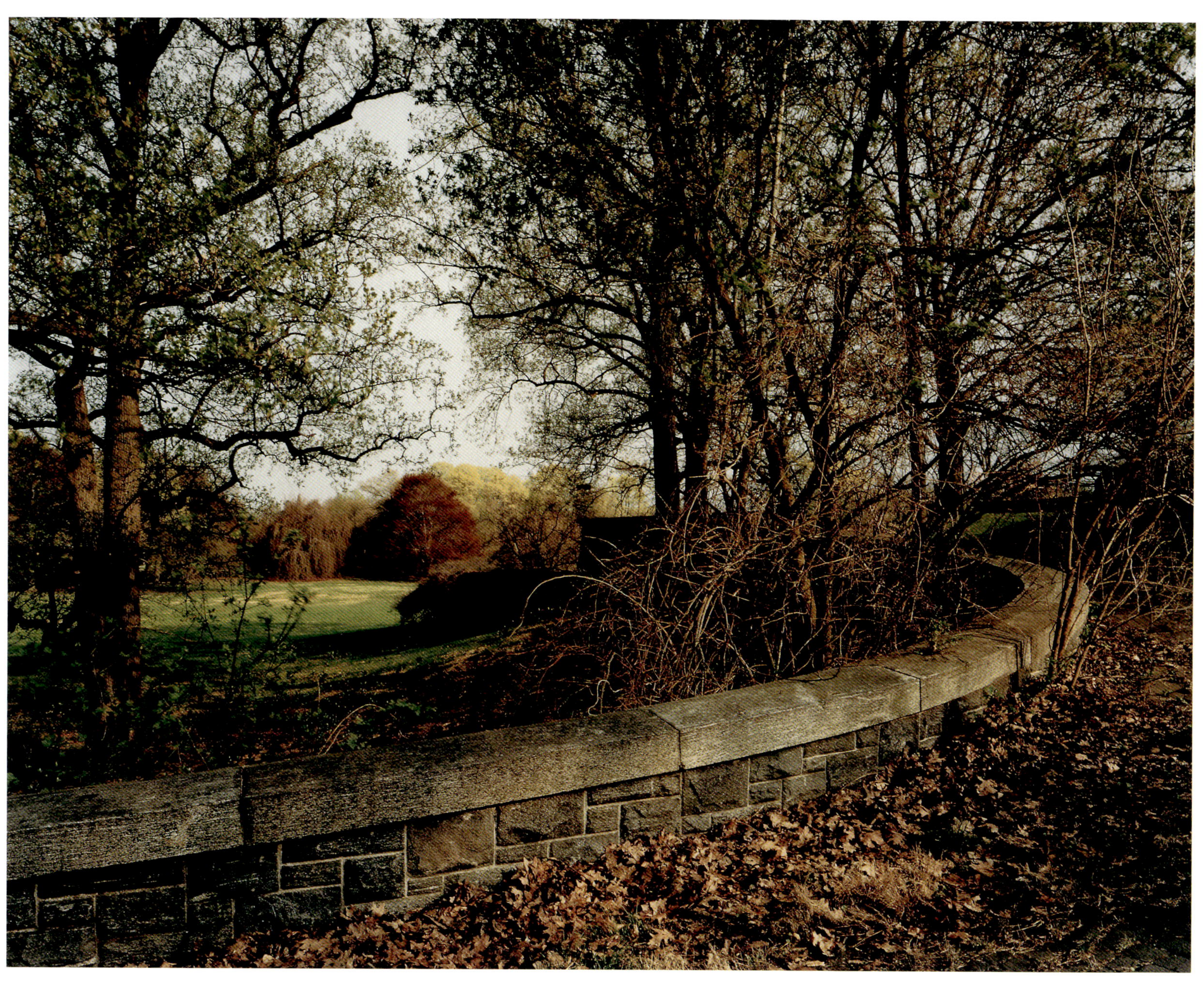

ROCKWOOD HALL, 1994

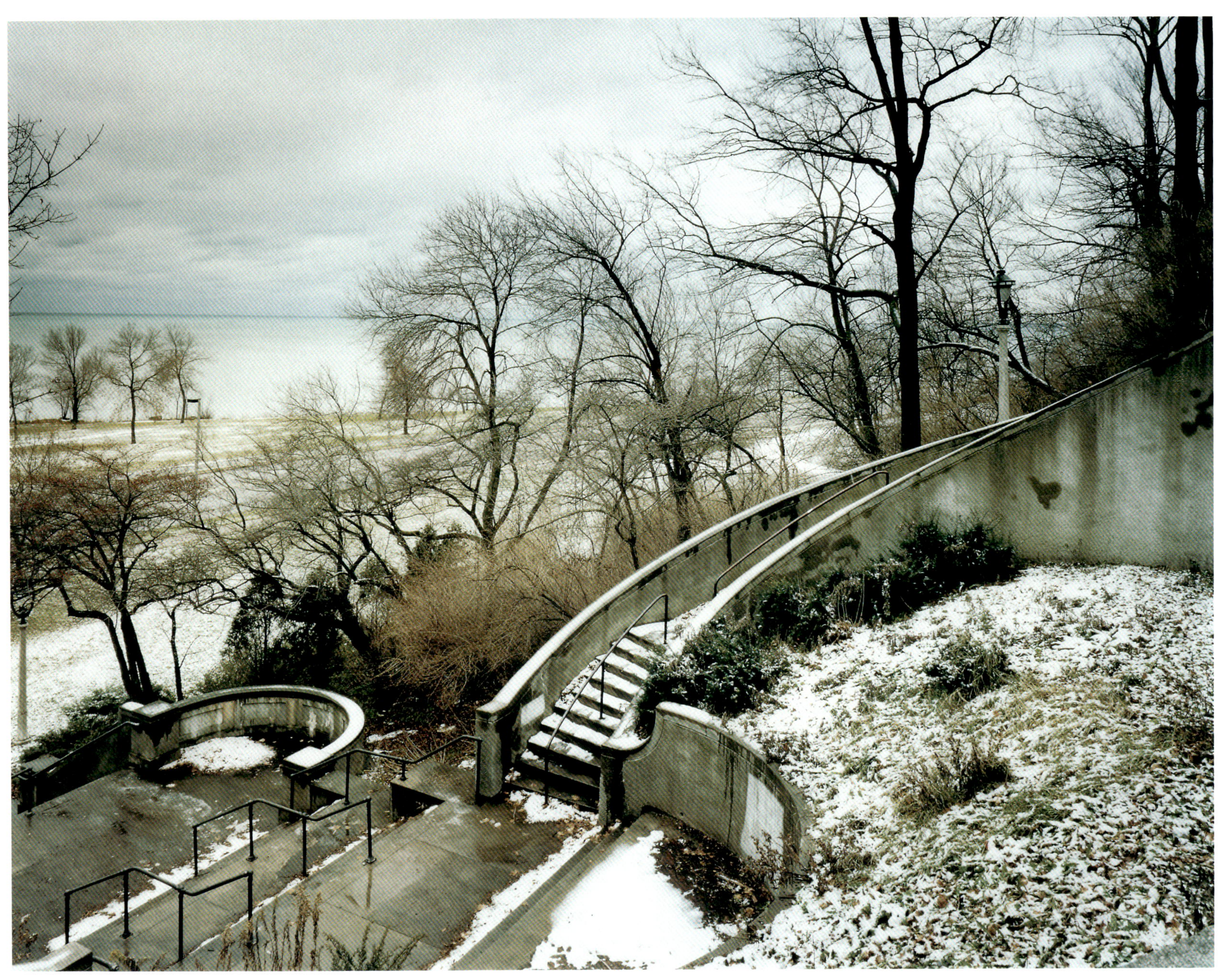

LAKE PARK, 1992

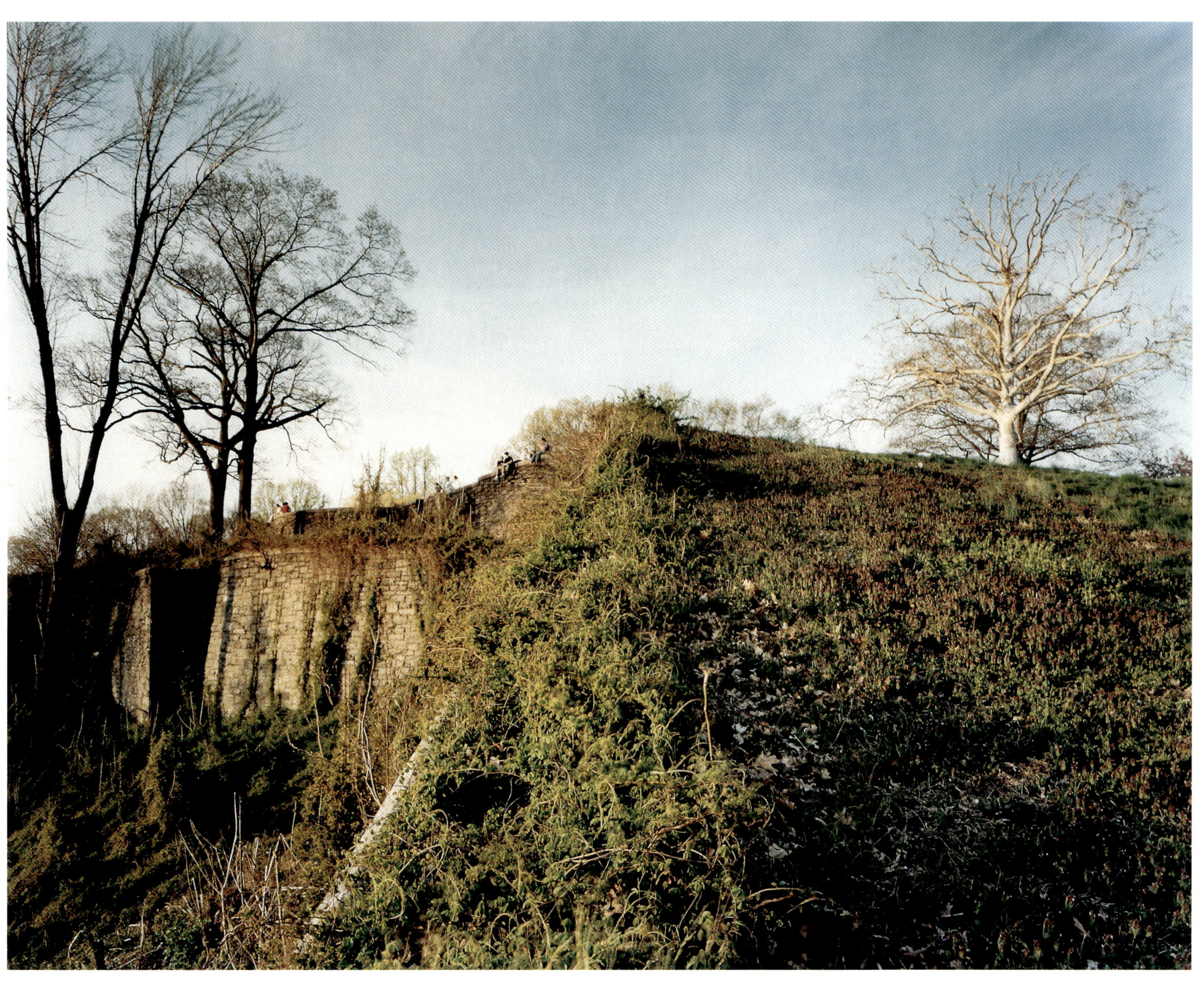

ROCKWOOD HALL, 1994

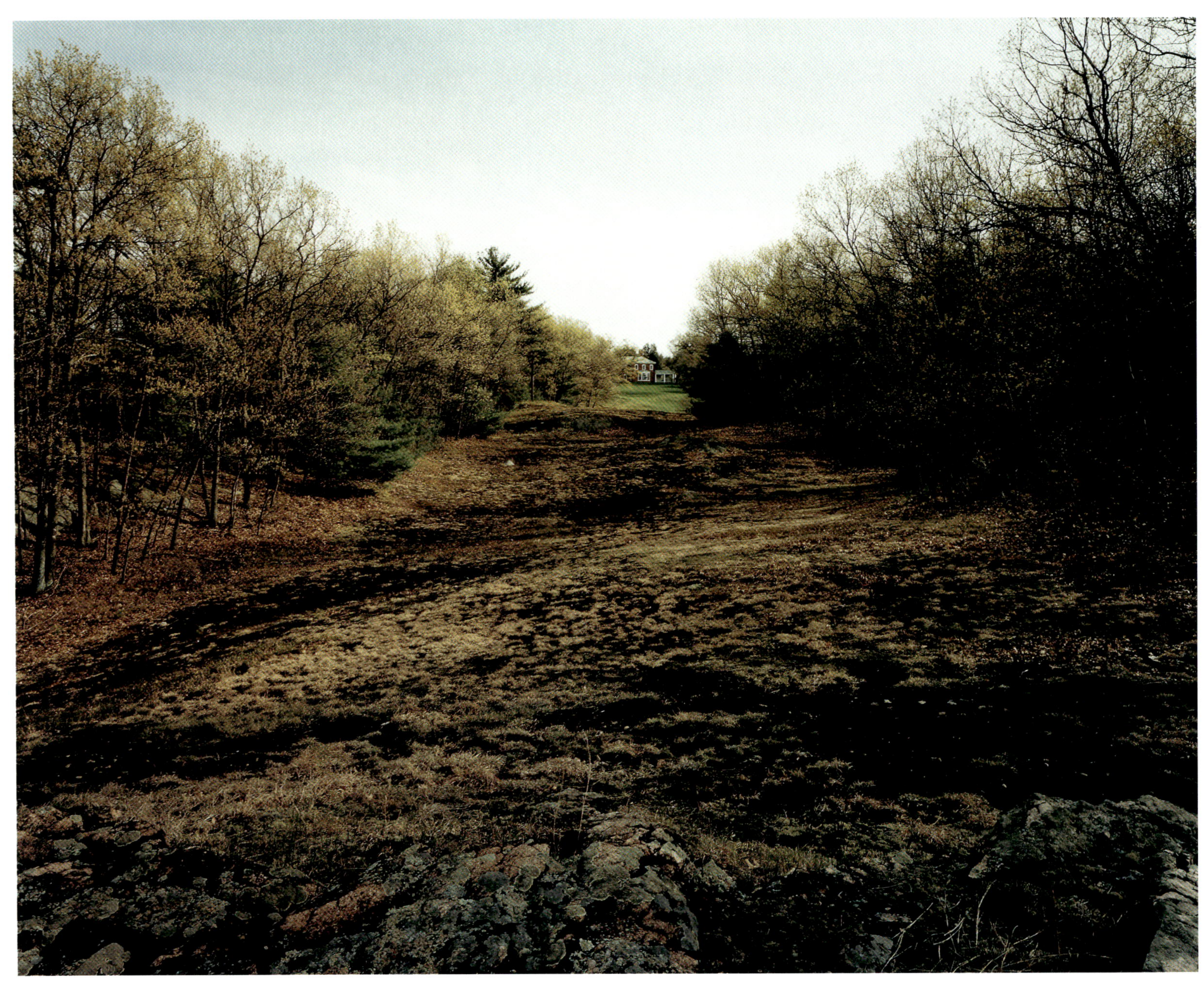

THE CEDARS, 1994

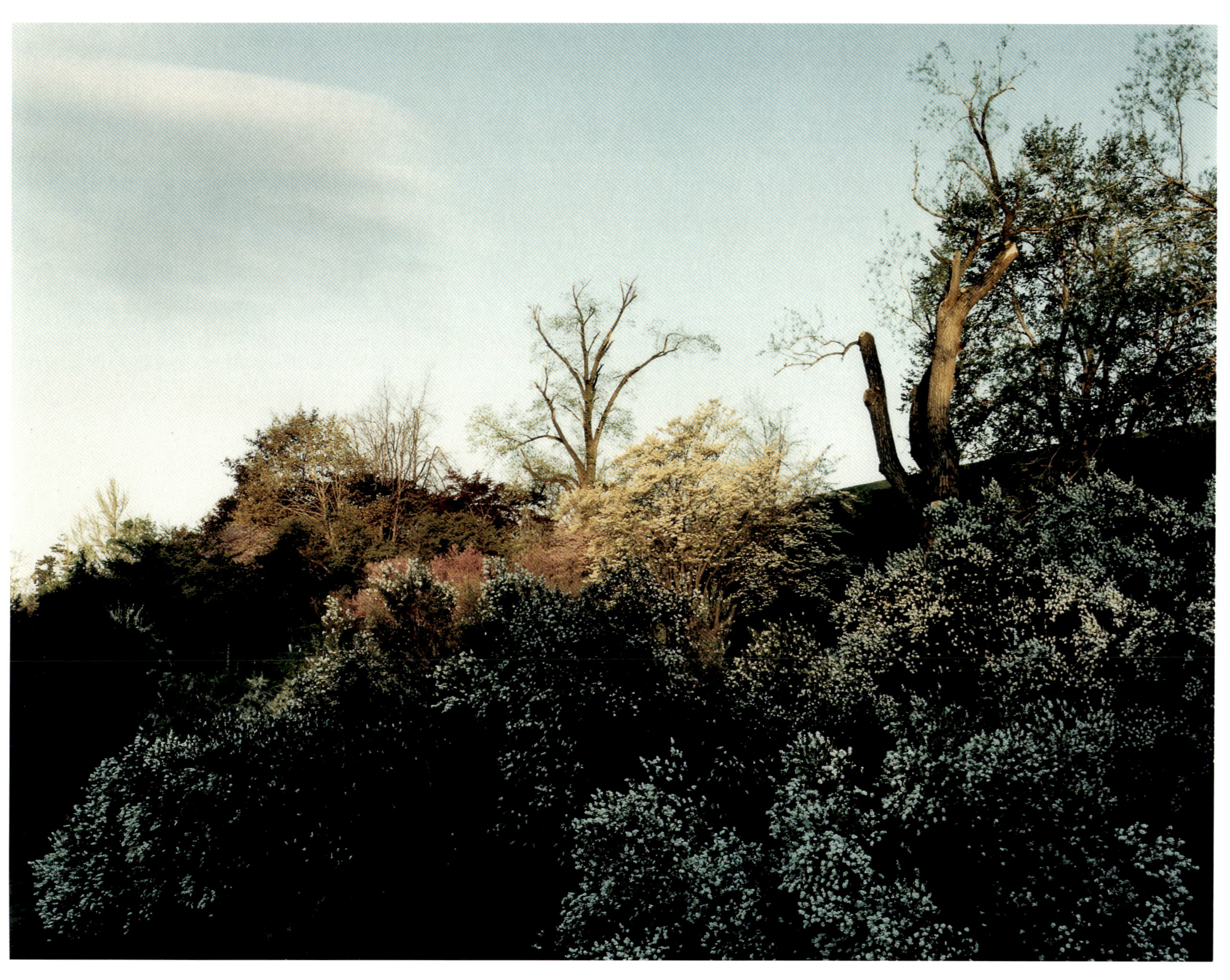

HIGHLAND PARK, 1991

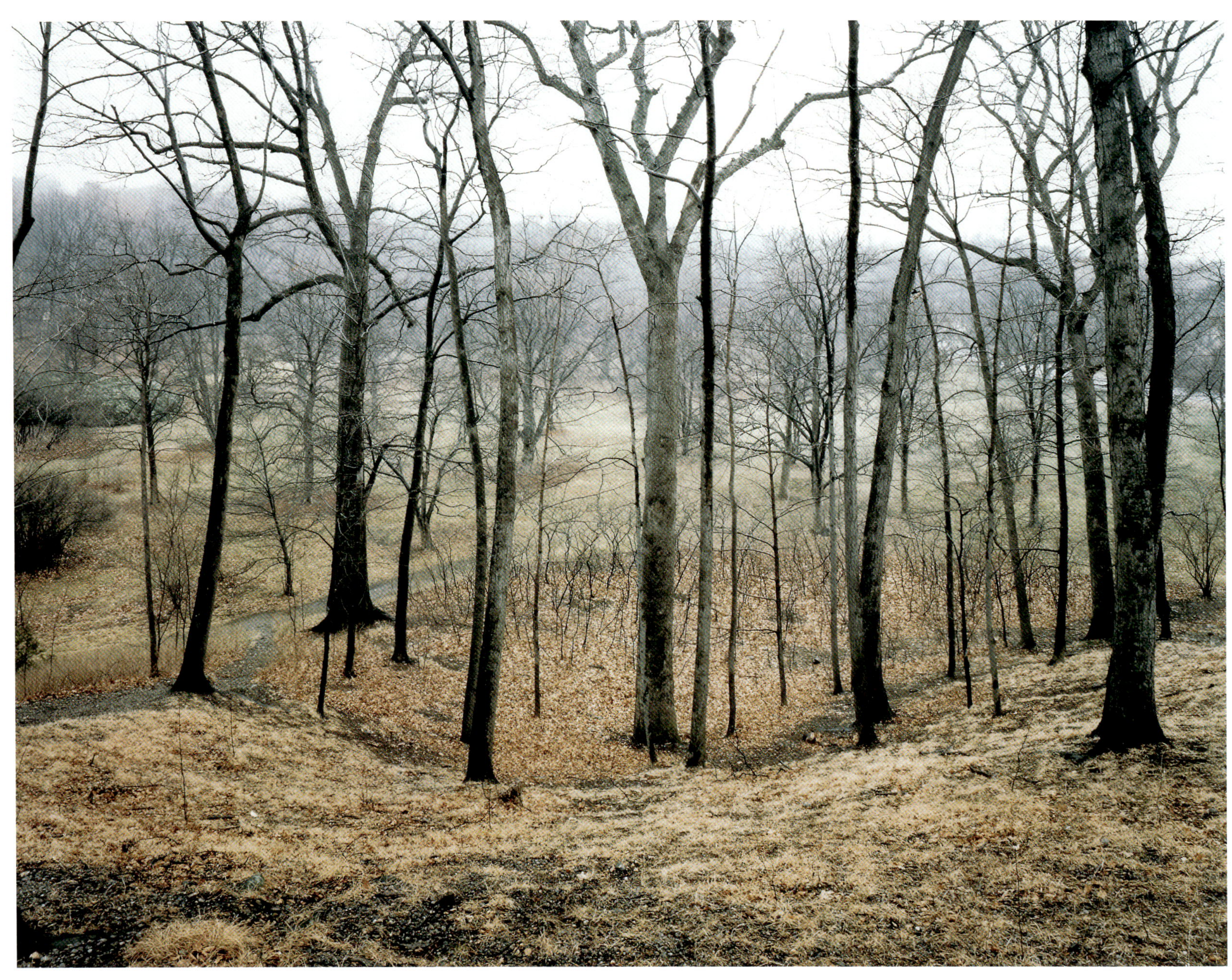

ARNOLD ARBORETUM, 1990

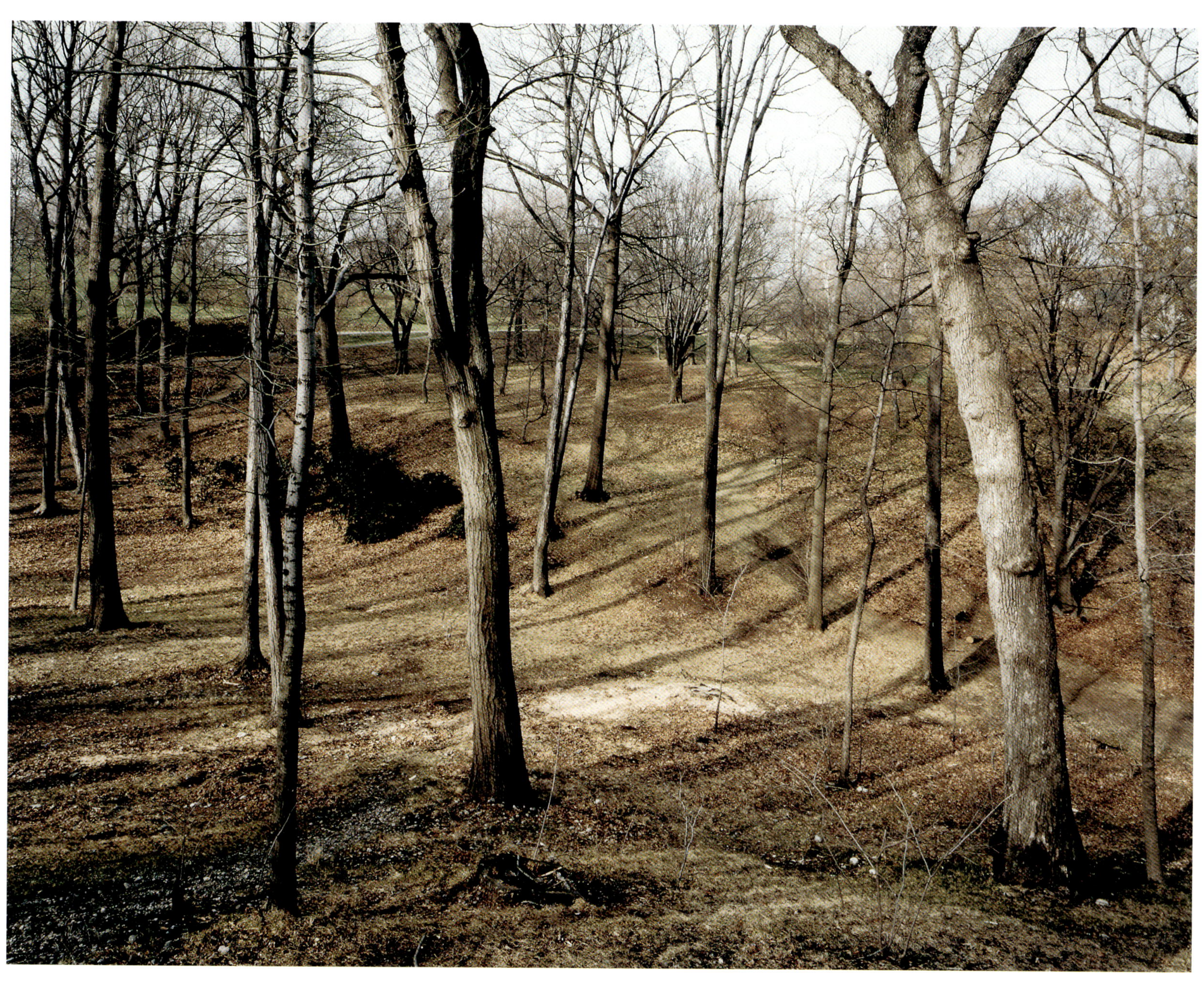

ARNOLD ARBORETUM, 1989

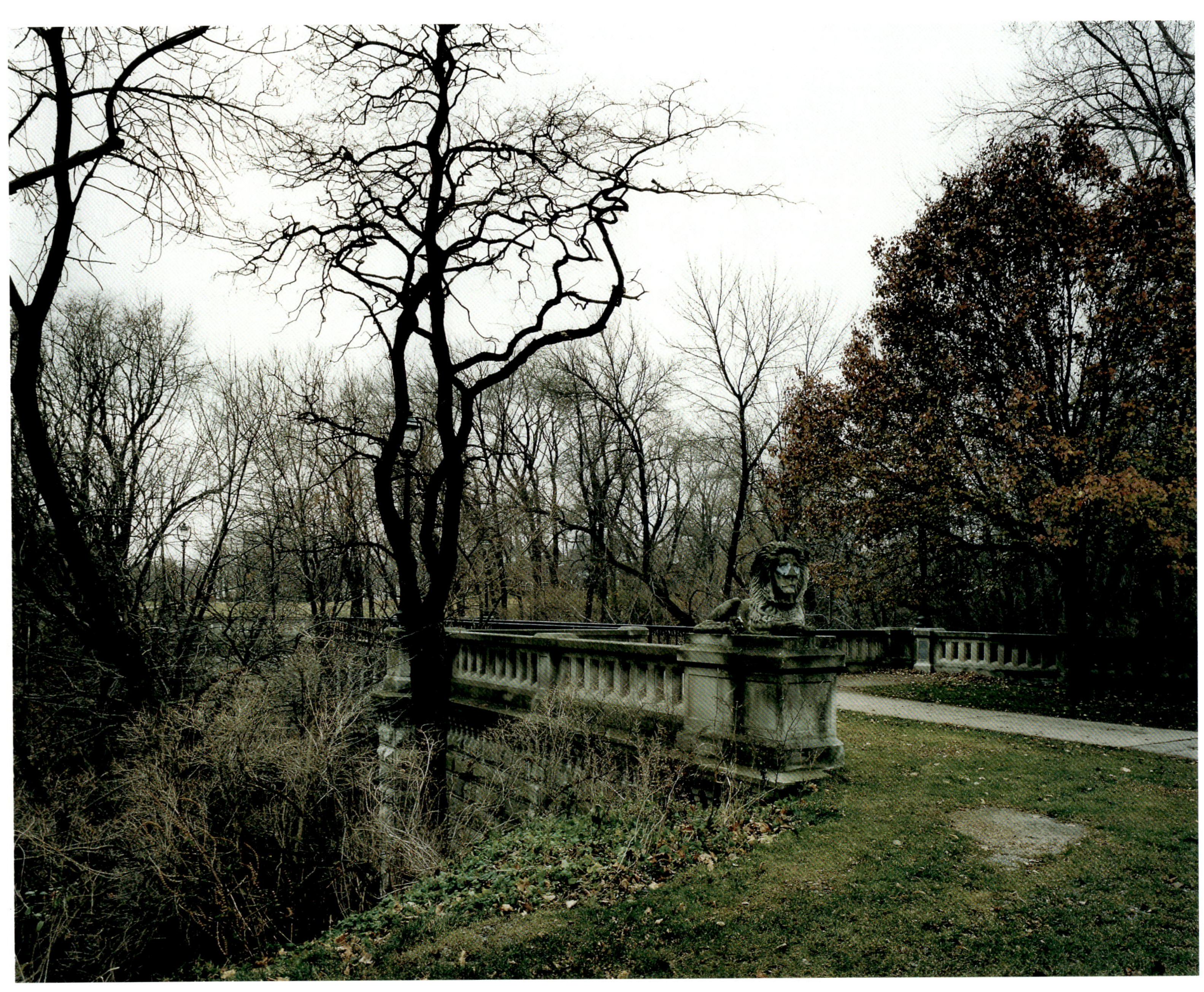

LAKE PARK, 1992

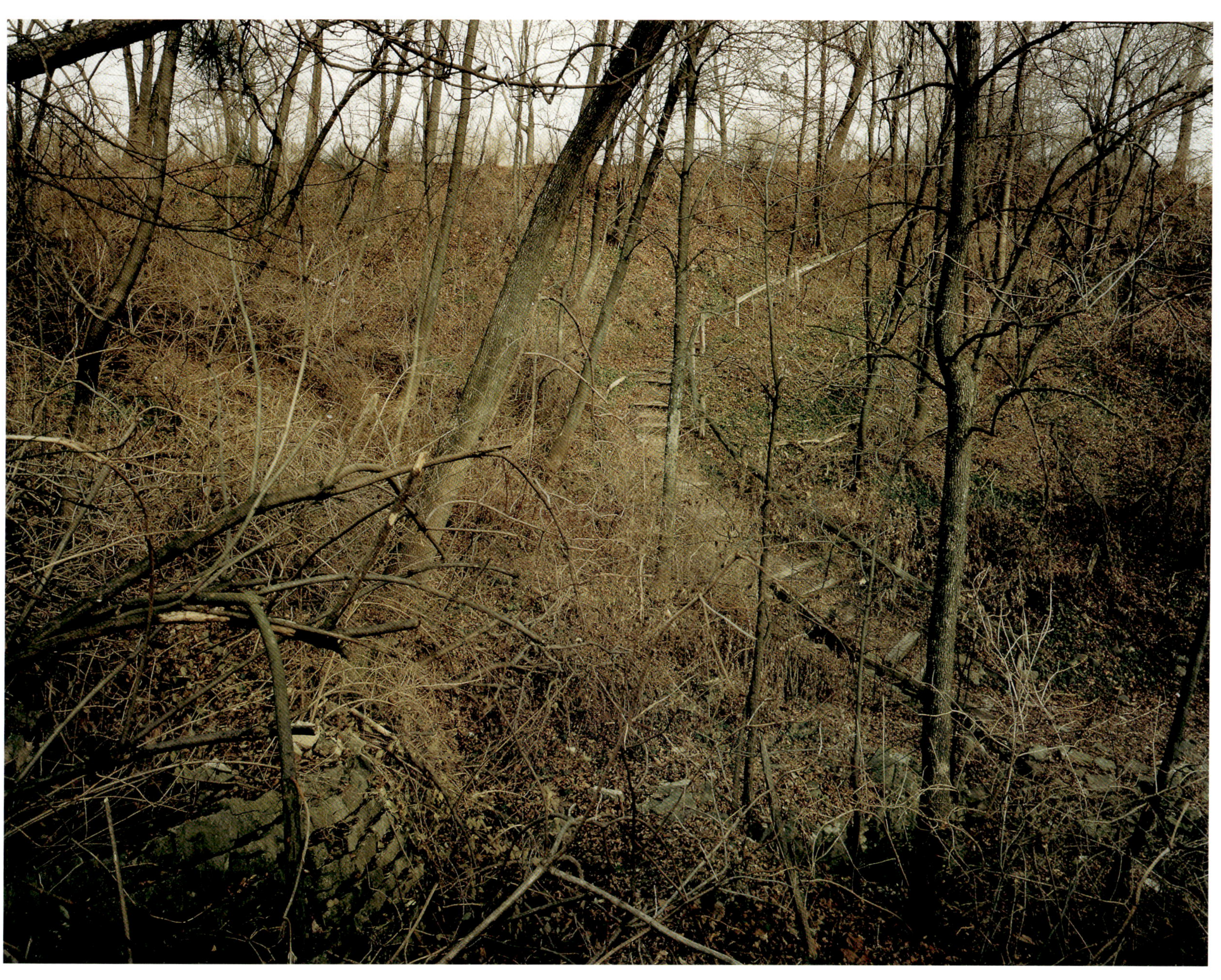

LAKE PARK, 1992

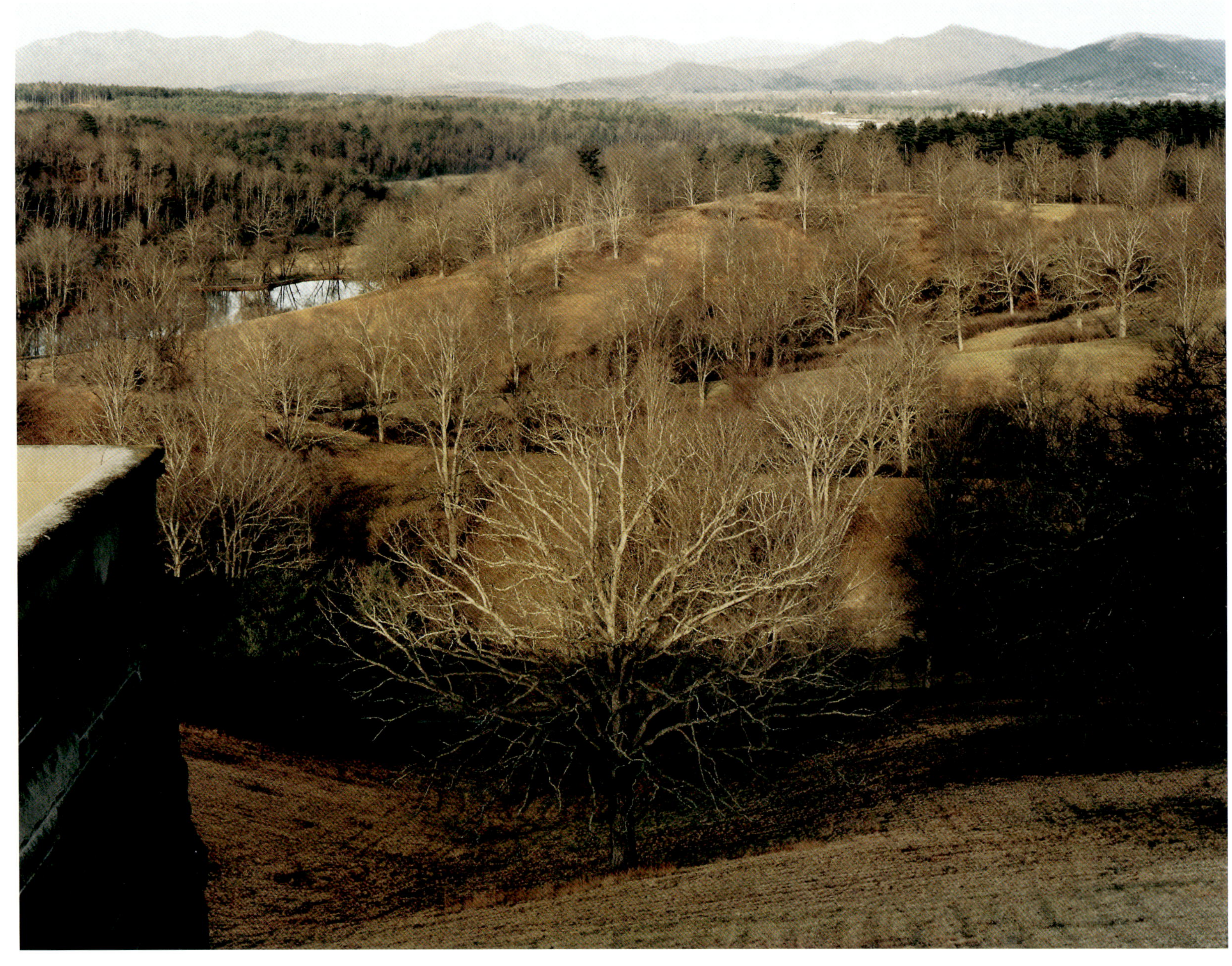

BILTMORE, 1993

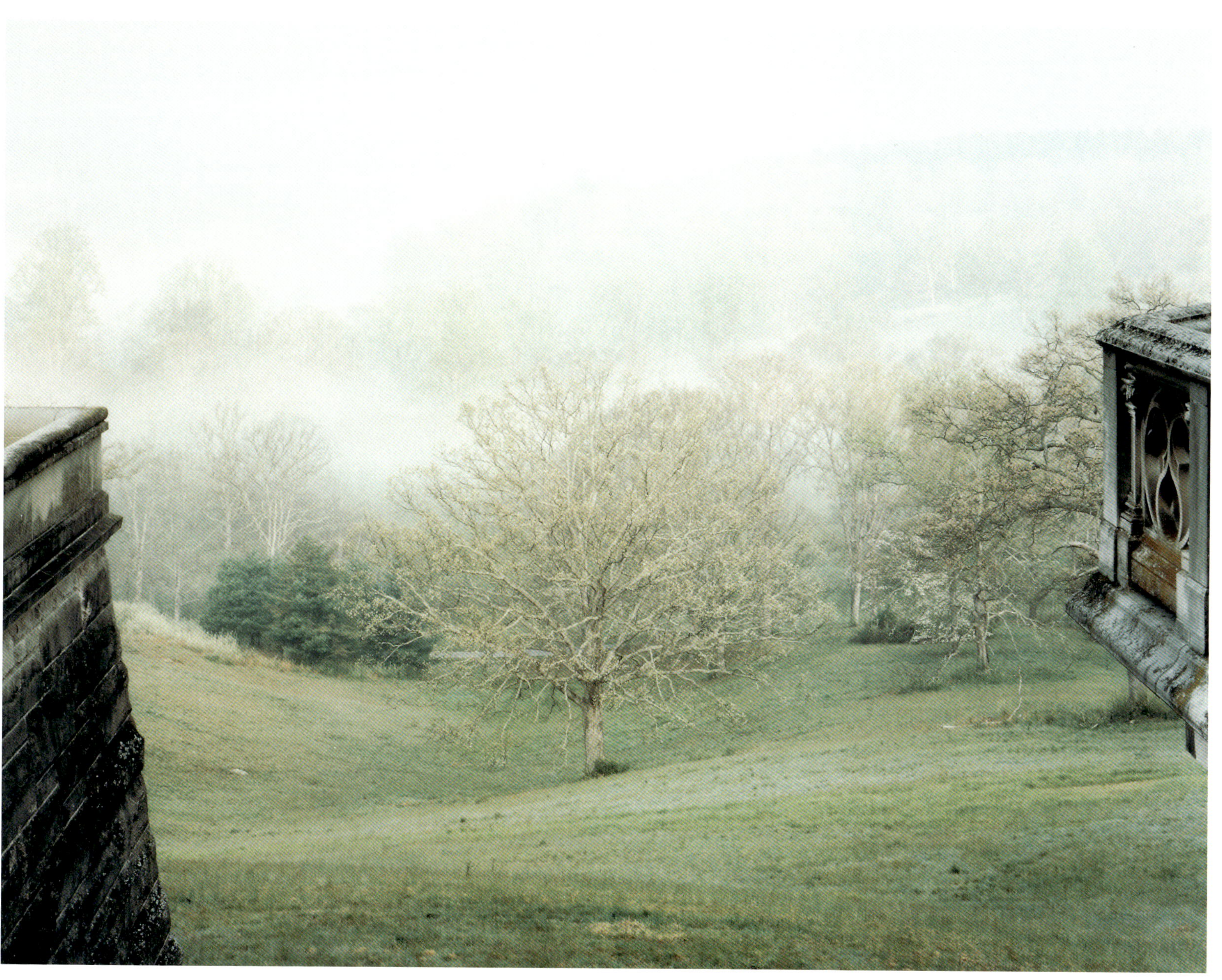

BILTMORE, 1990

LEE FRIEDLANDER

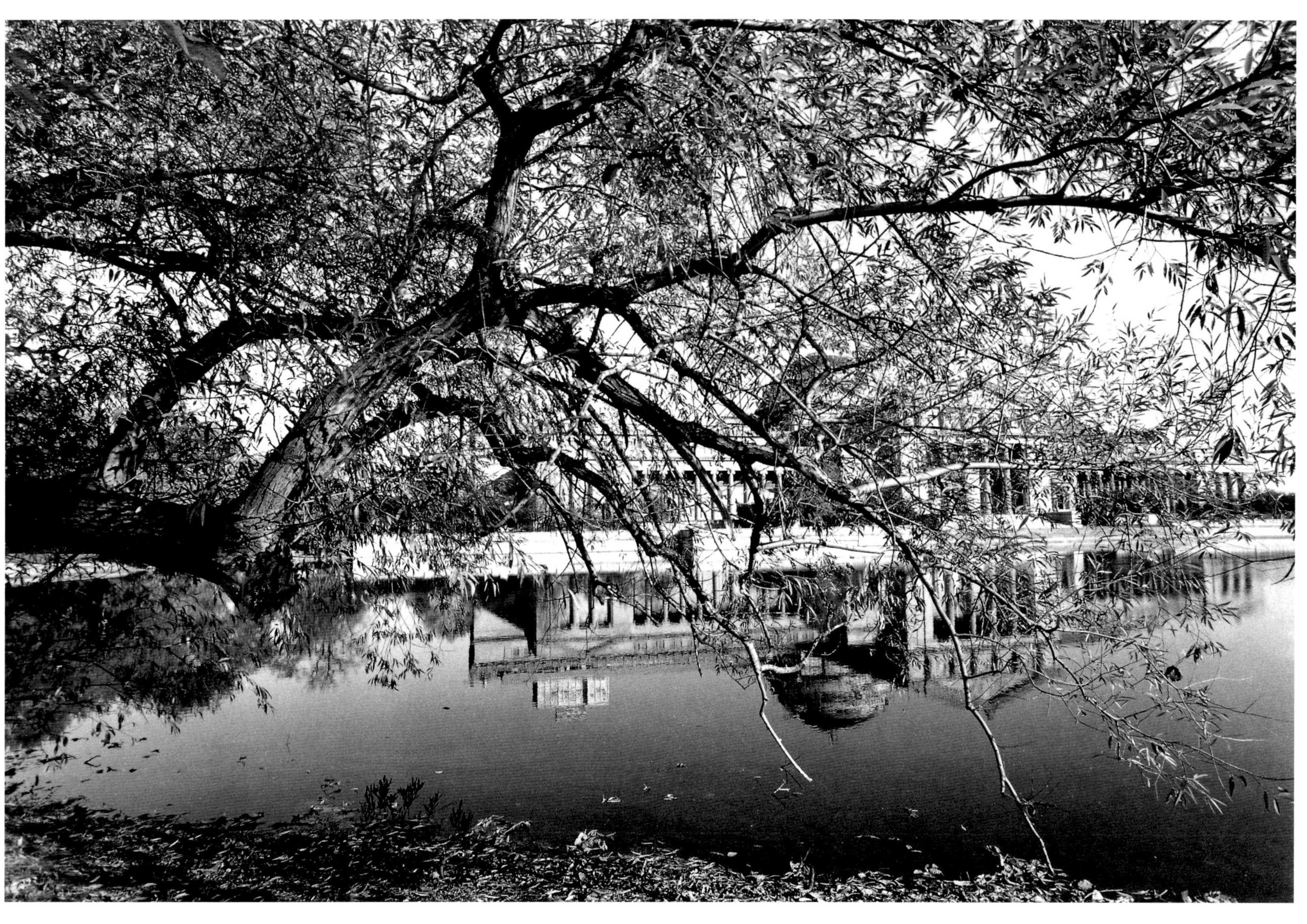

JACKSON PARK, 1988

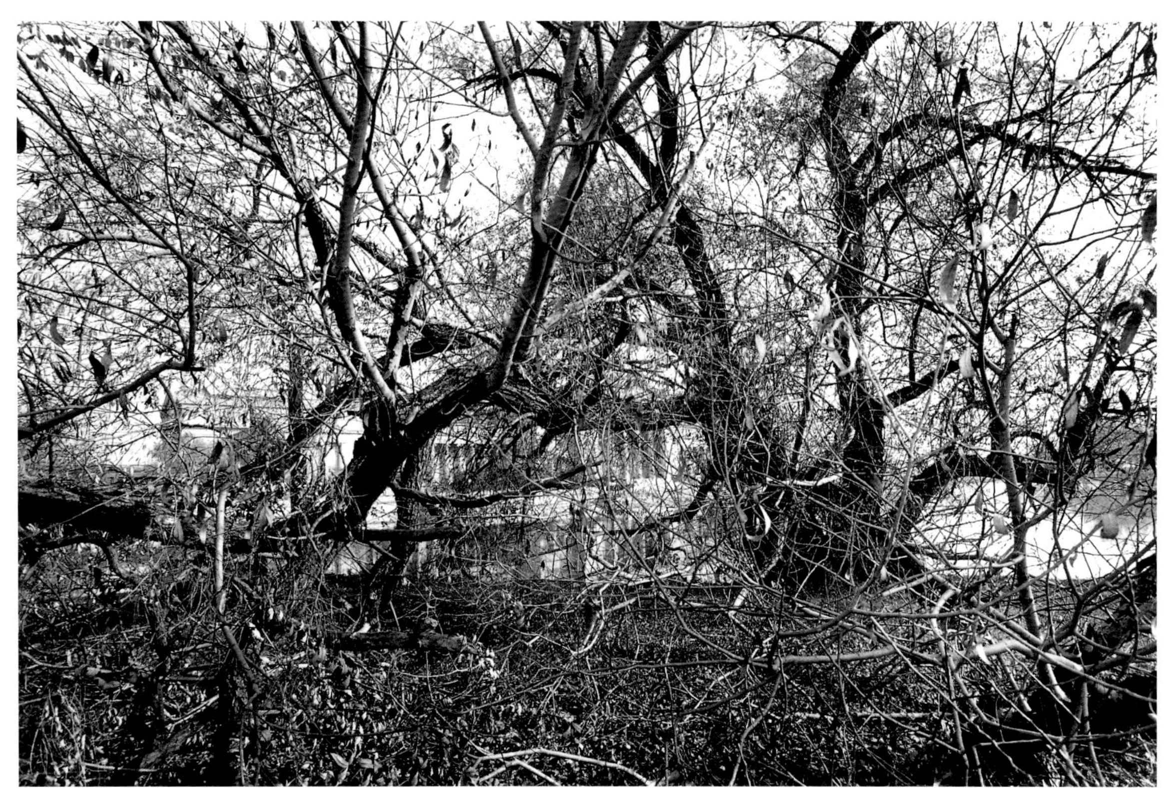

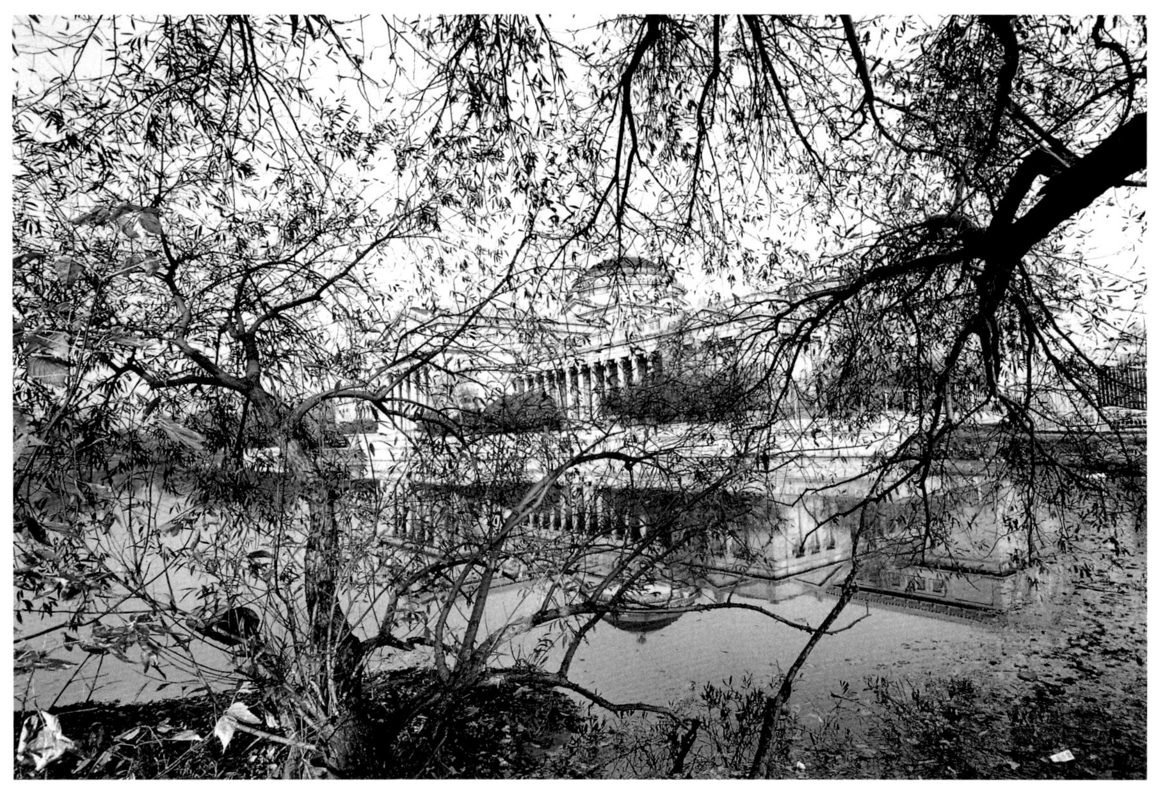

JACKSON PARK, 1989

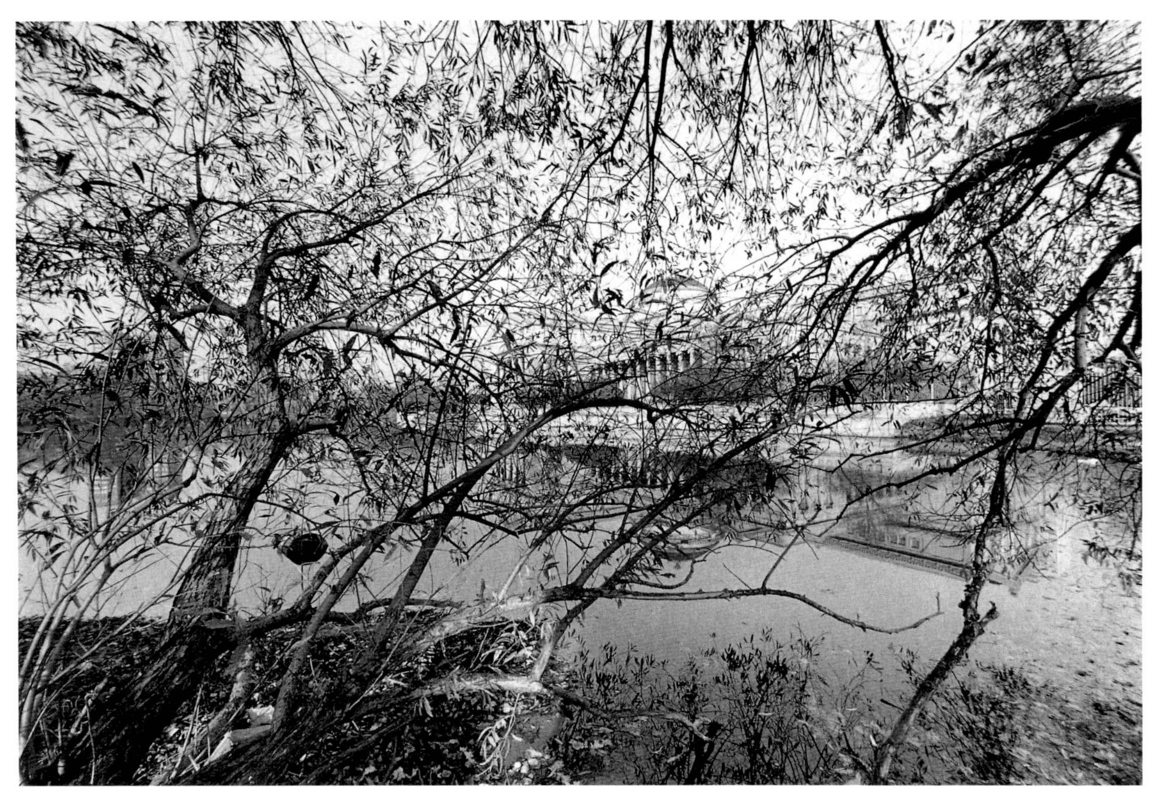

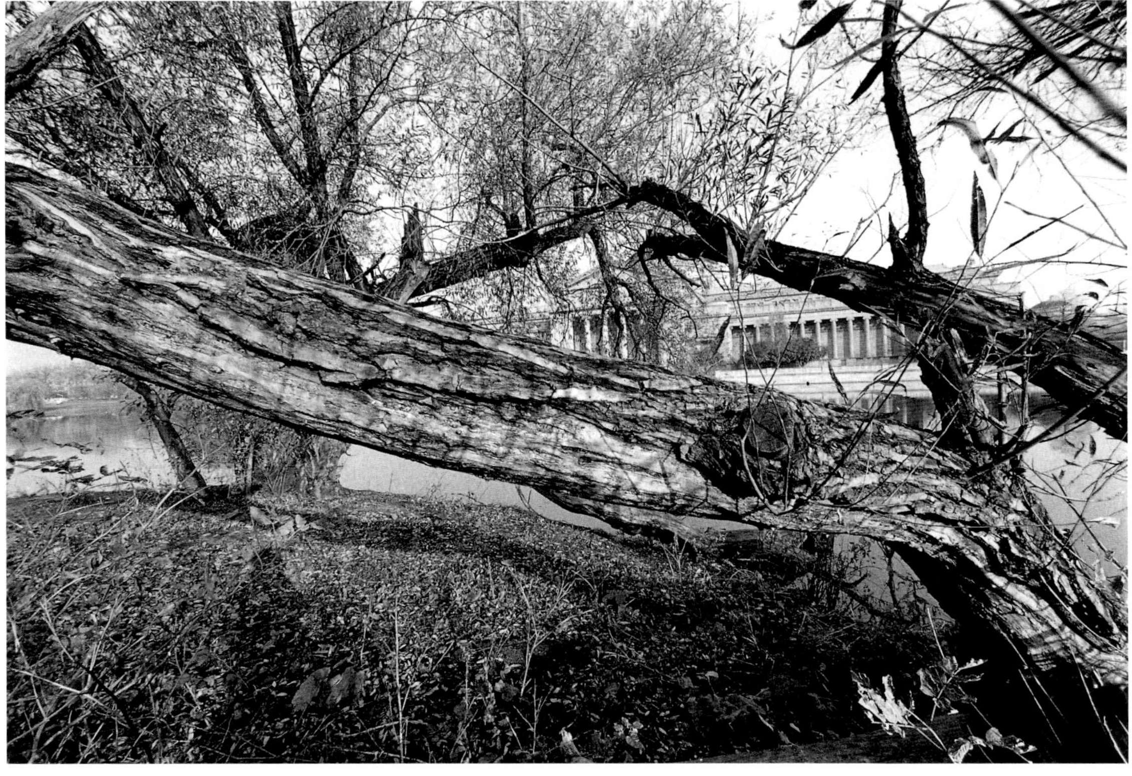

JACKSON PARK, 1989

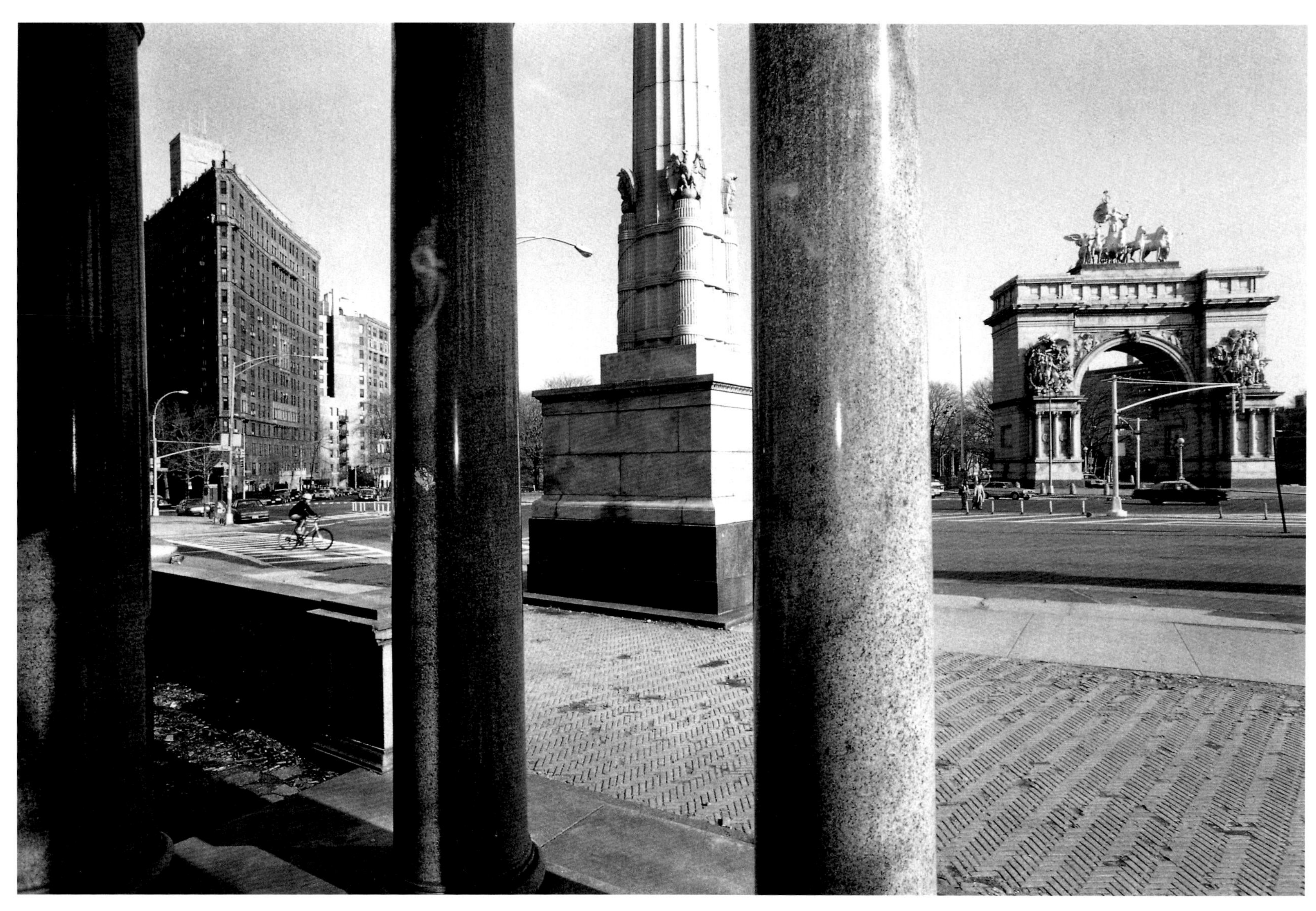

GRAND ARMY PLAZA, 1989

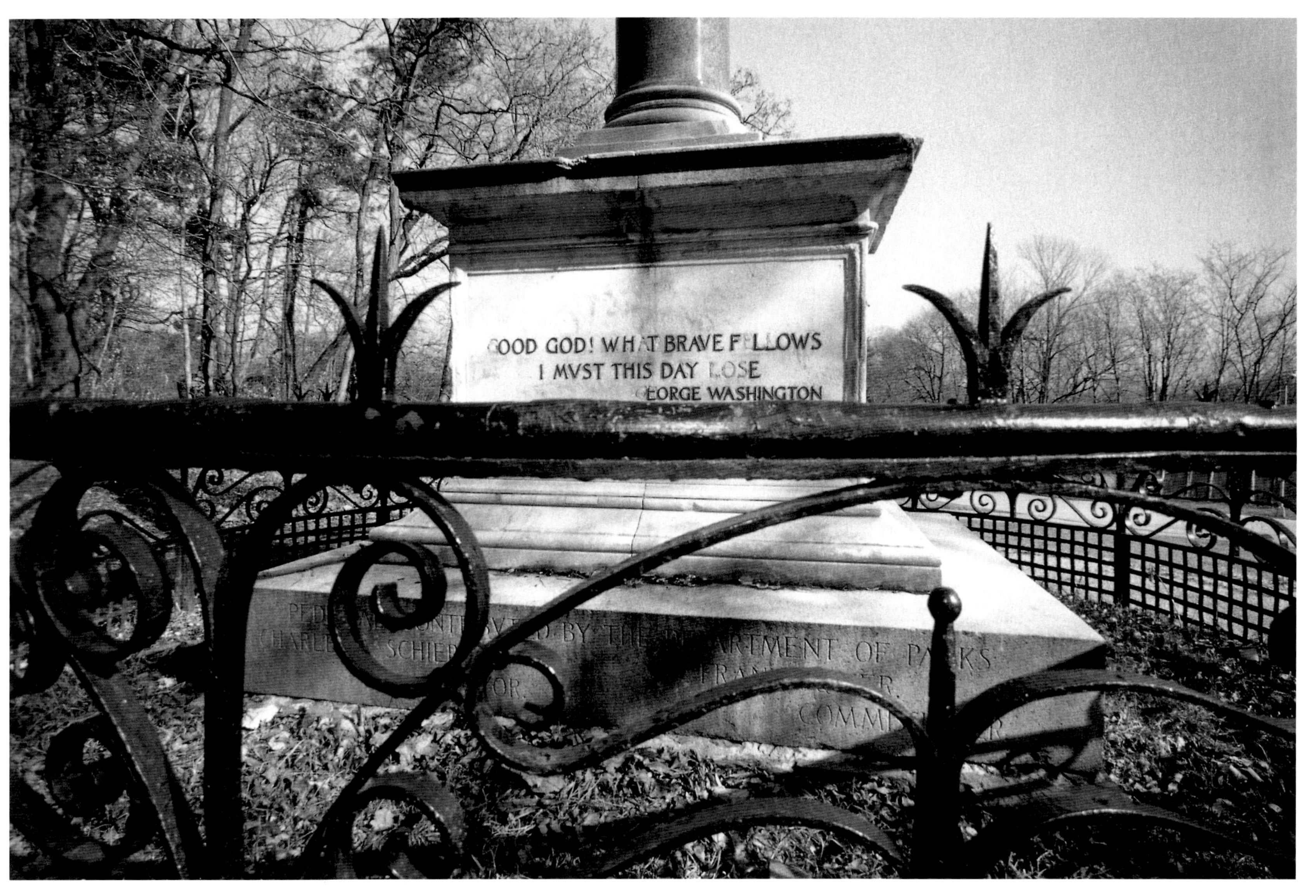

PROSPECT PARK, 1990

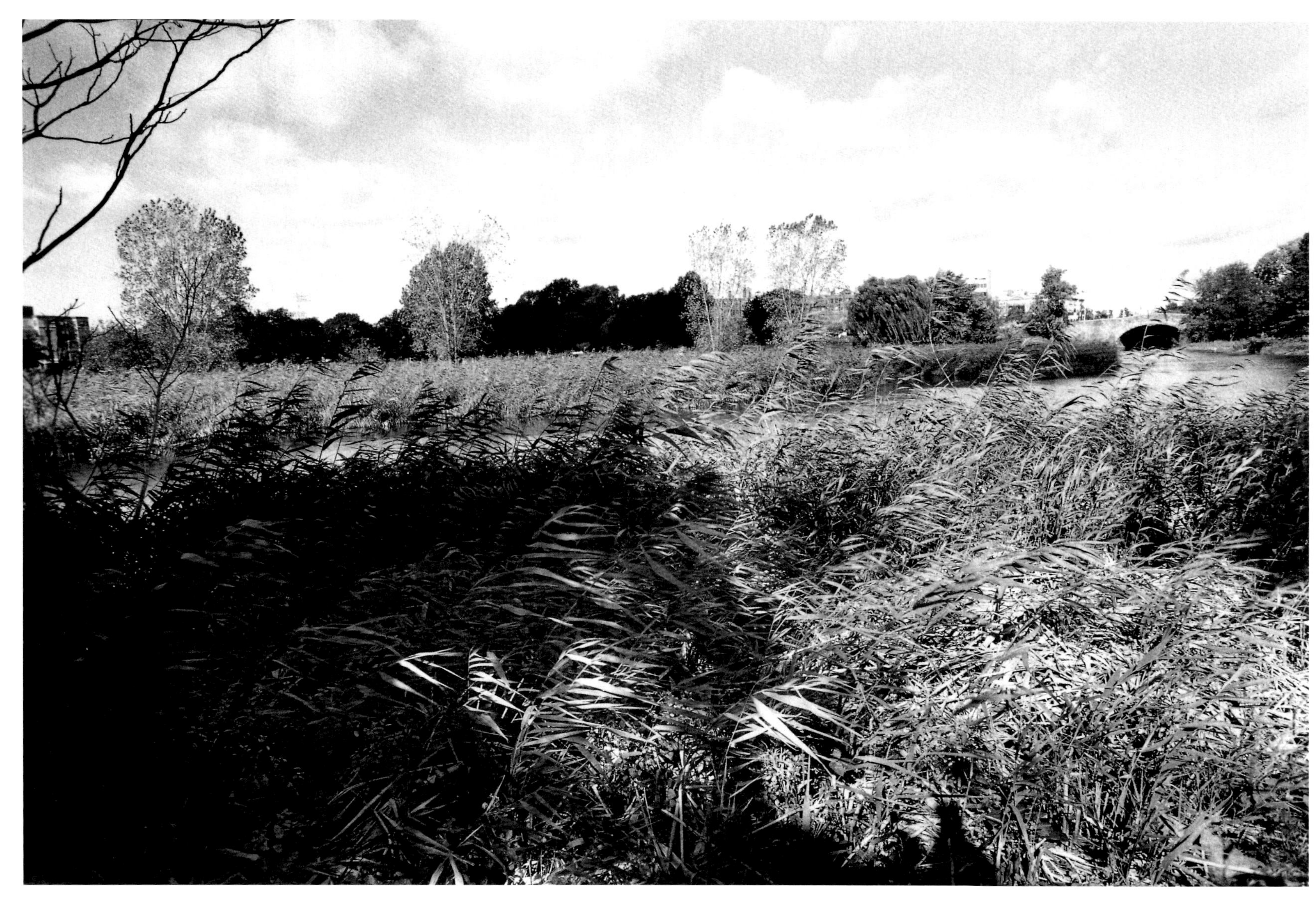

THE BACK BAY FENS, 1990

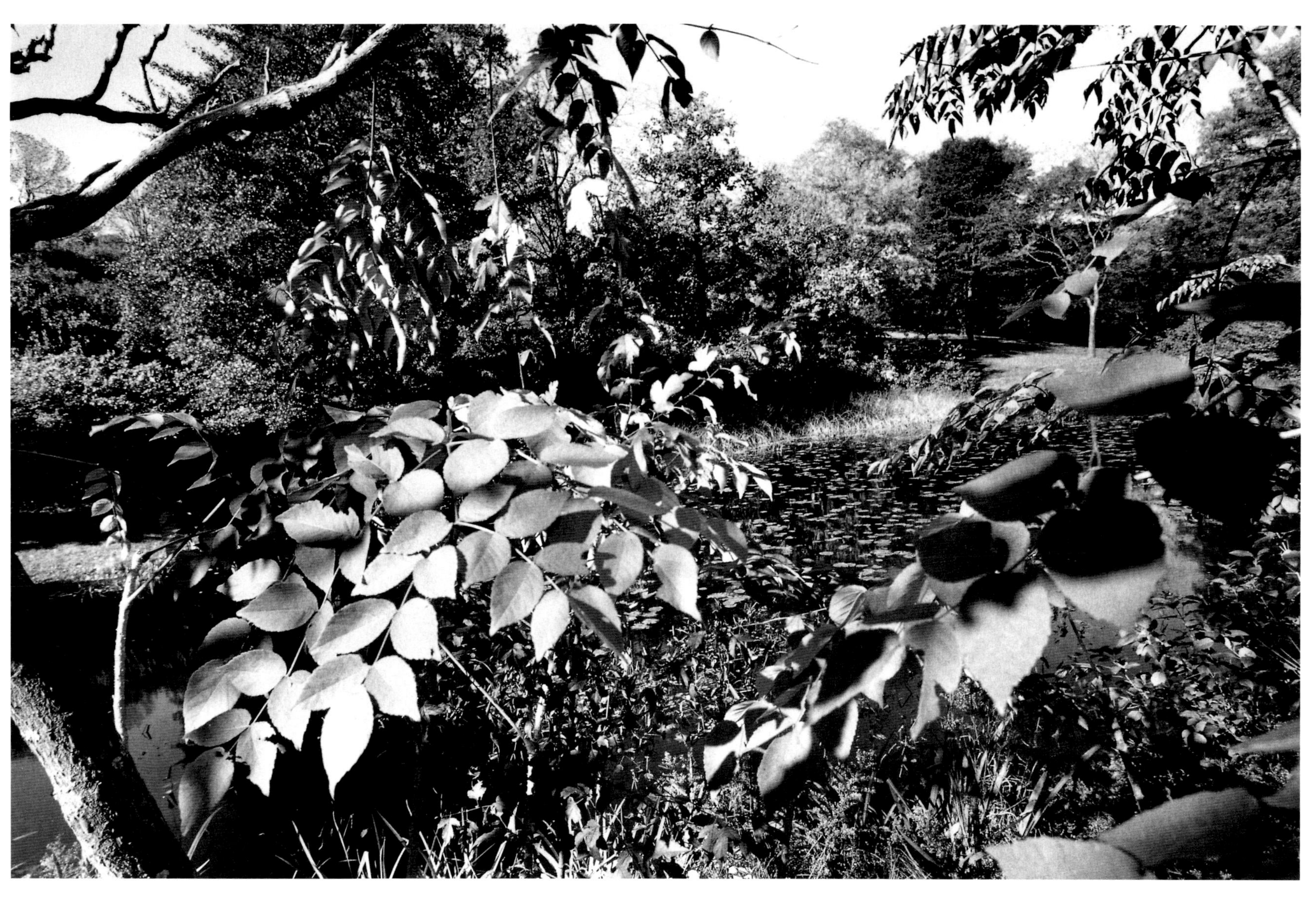

ARNOLD ARBORETUM, 1990

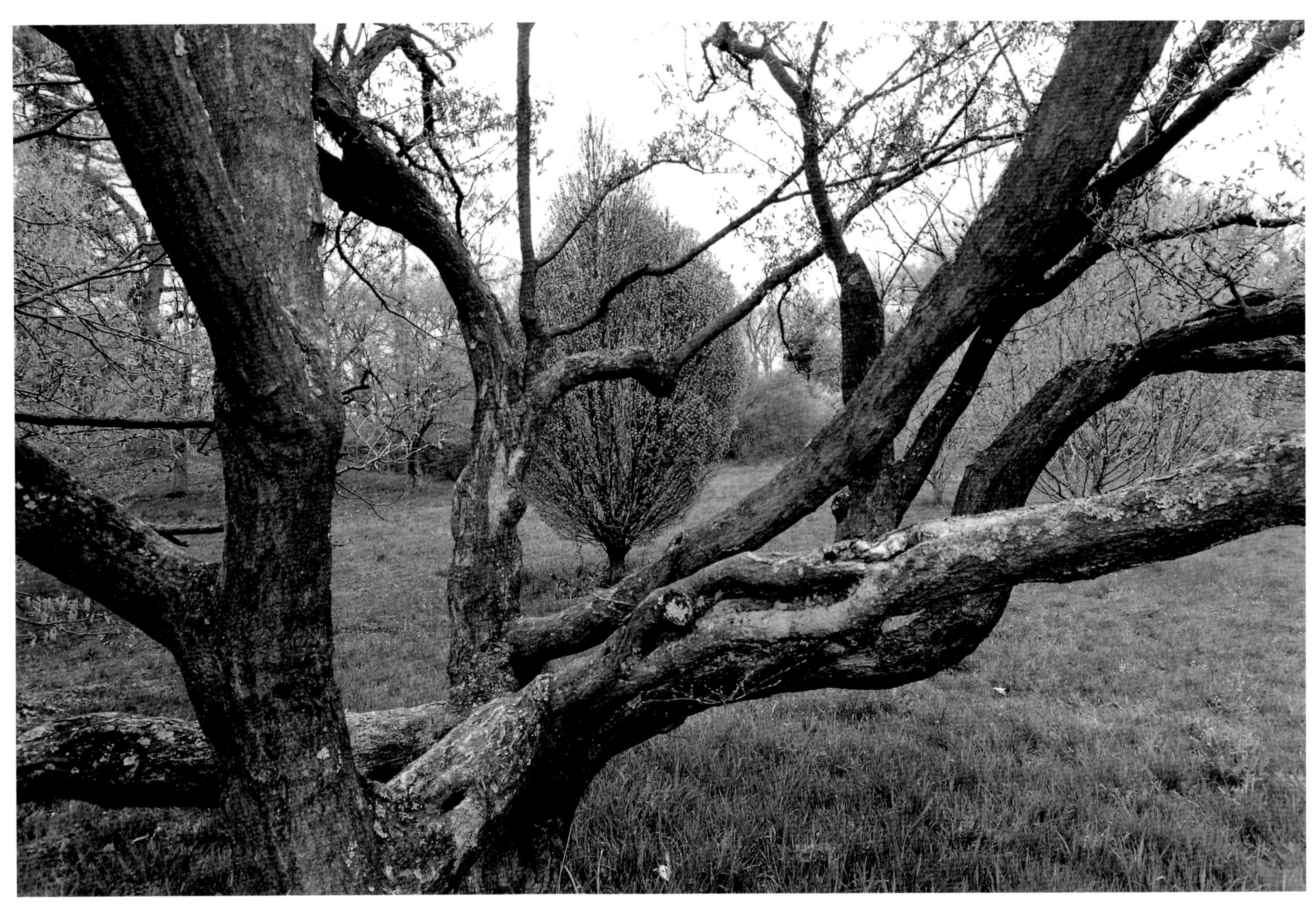

ARNOLD ARBORETUM, 1988

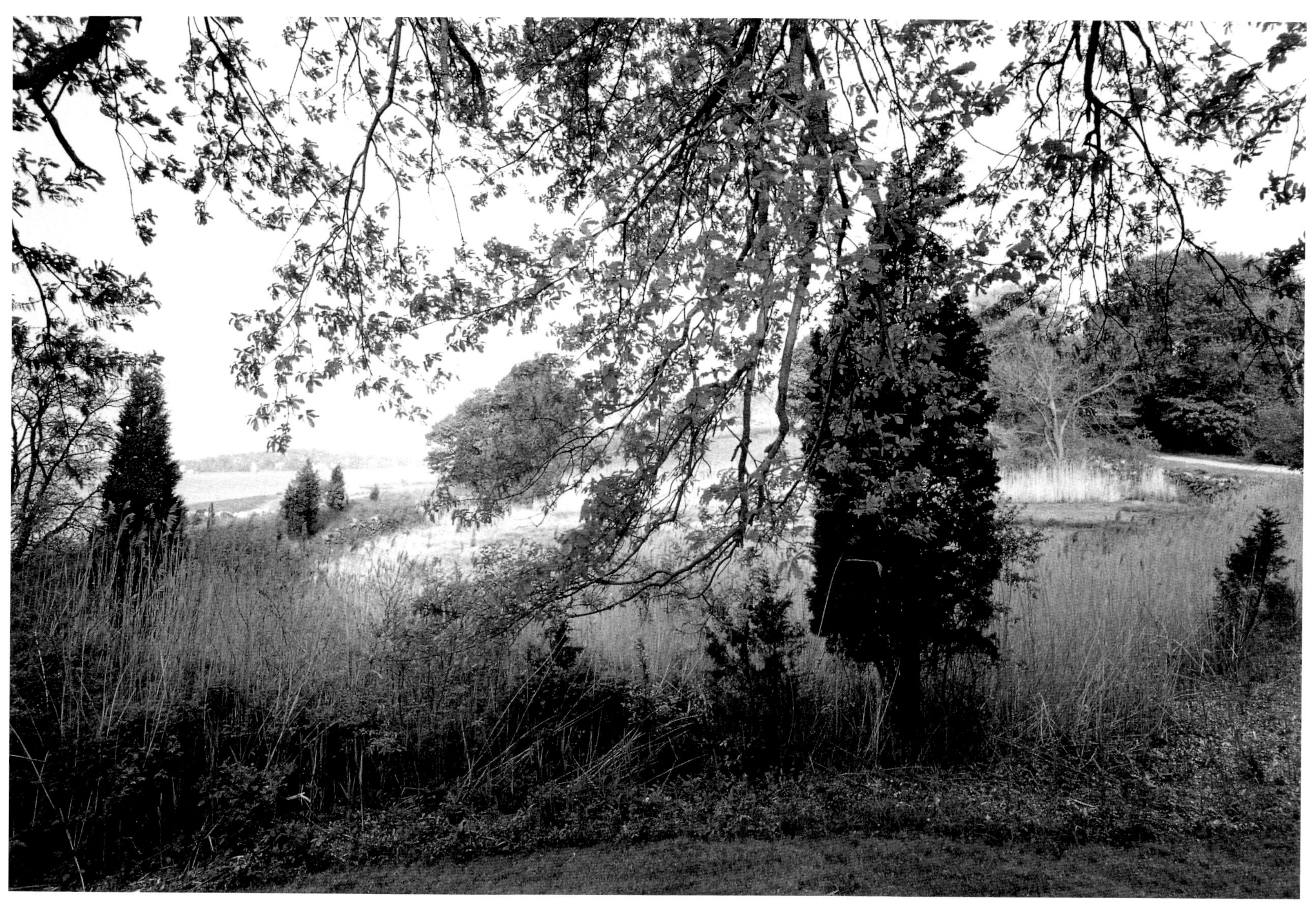

WORLD'S END, 1991

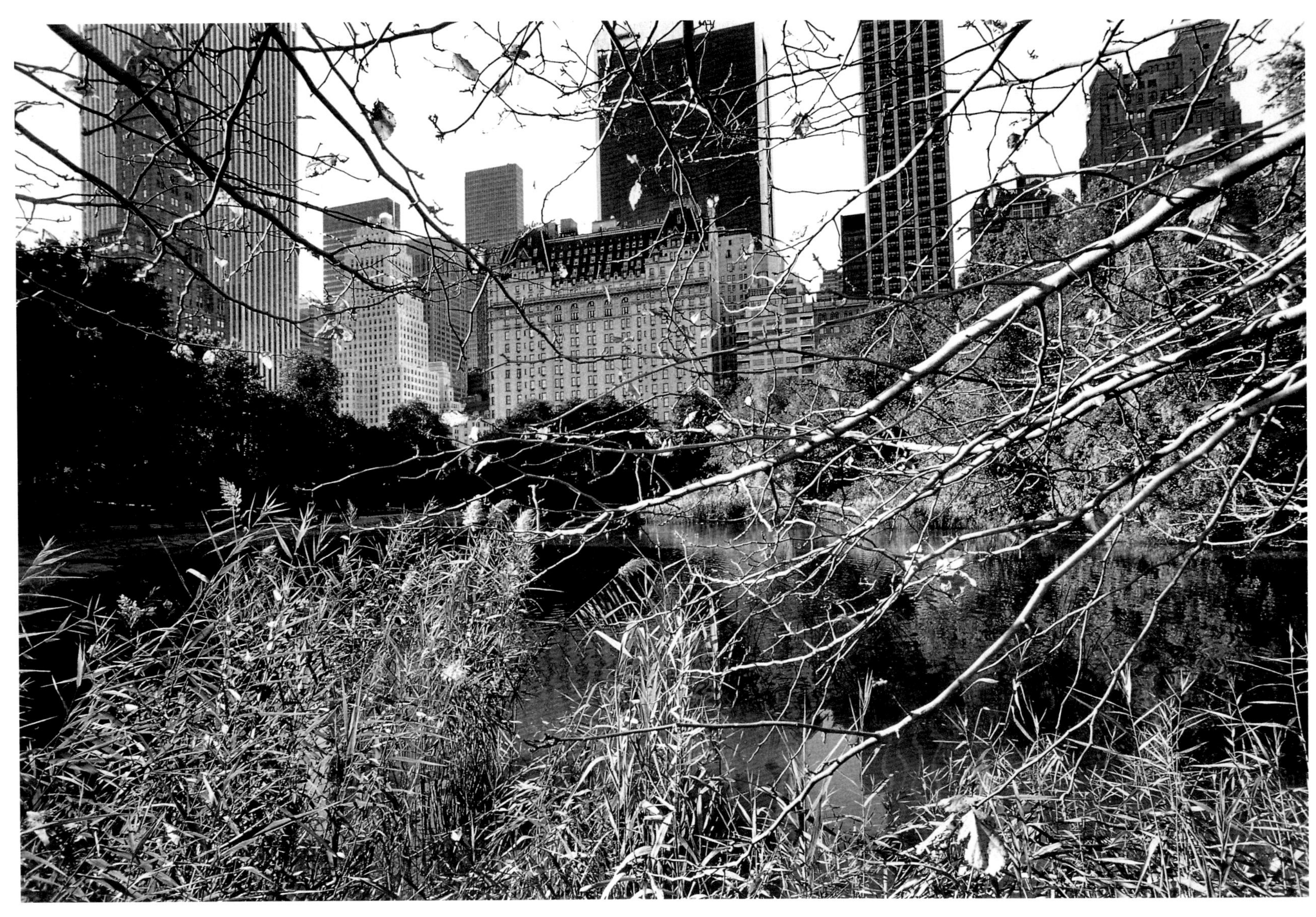

CENTRAL PARK, 1991

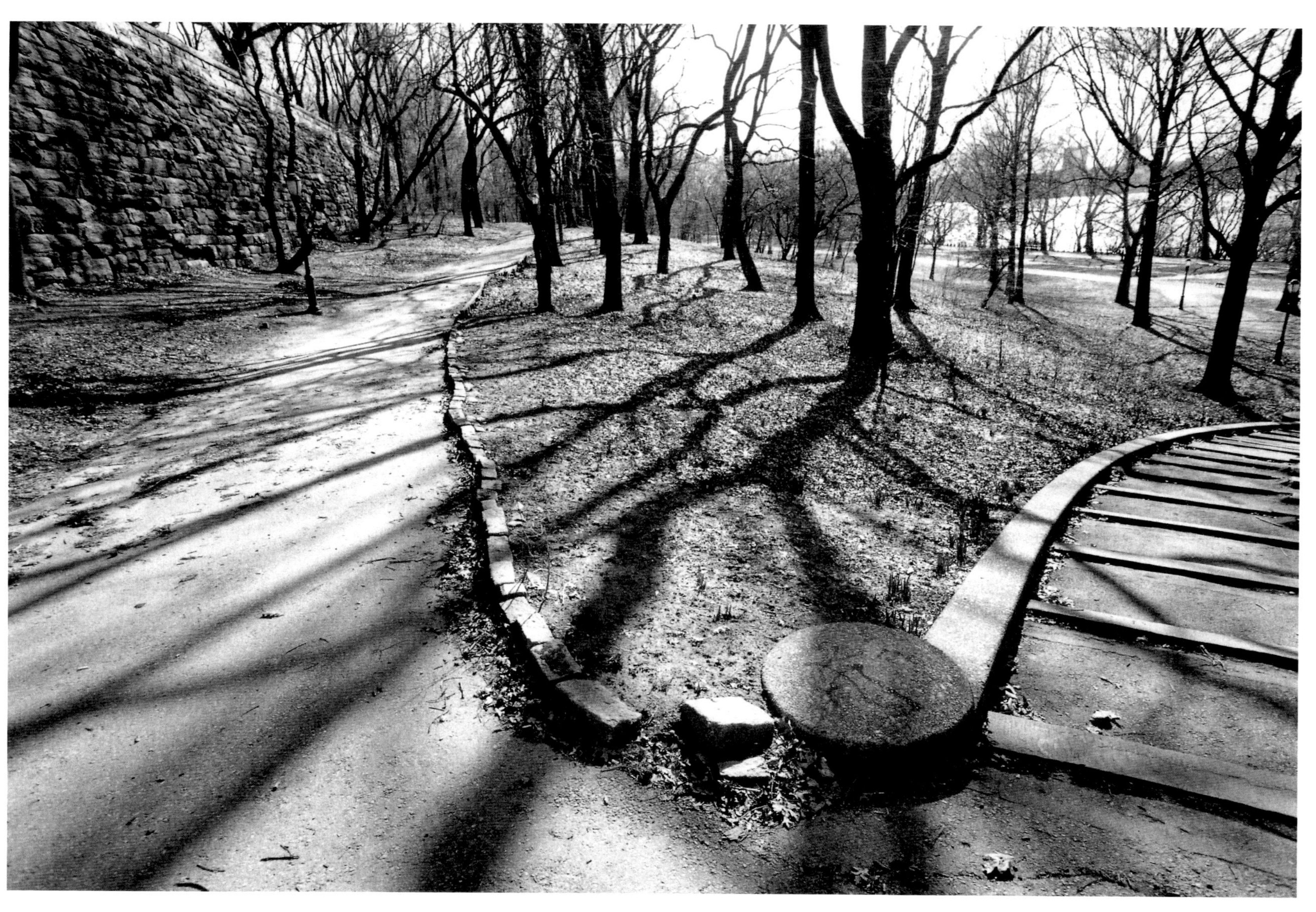

RIVERSIDE PARK, 1991

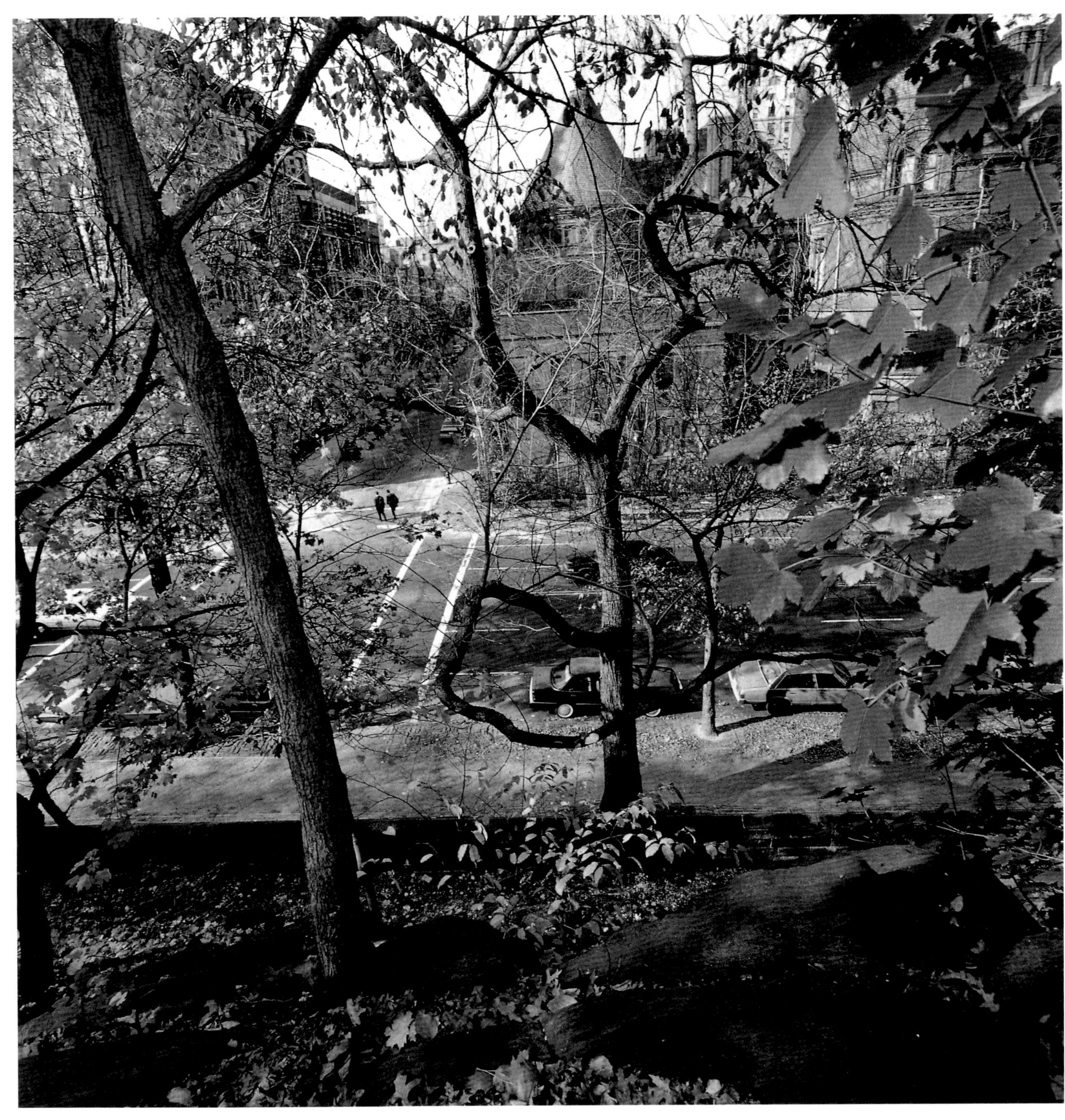

CENTRAL PARK, 1993

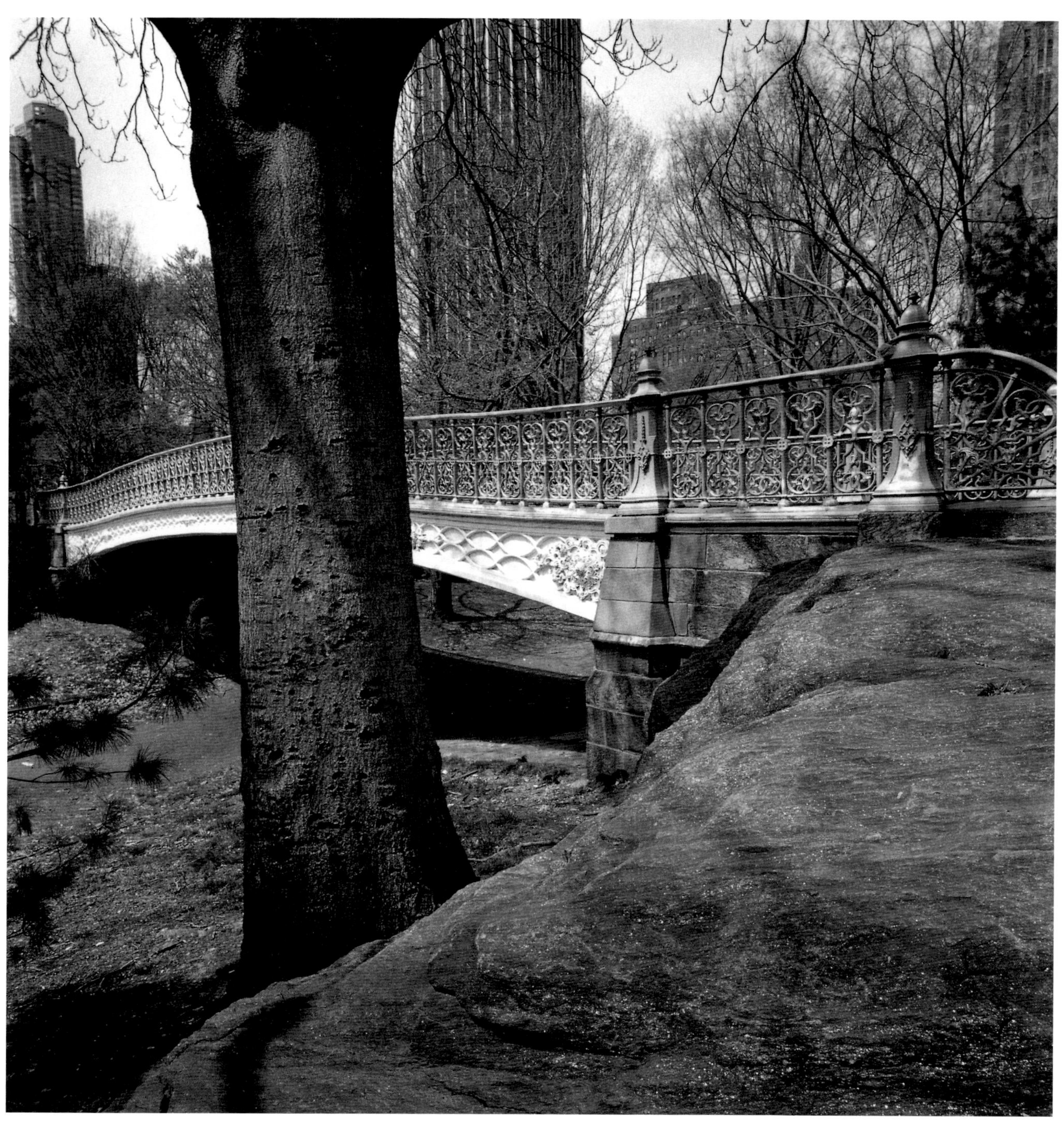

CENTRAL PARK, 1994

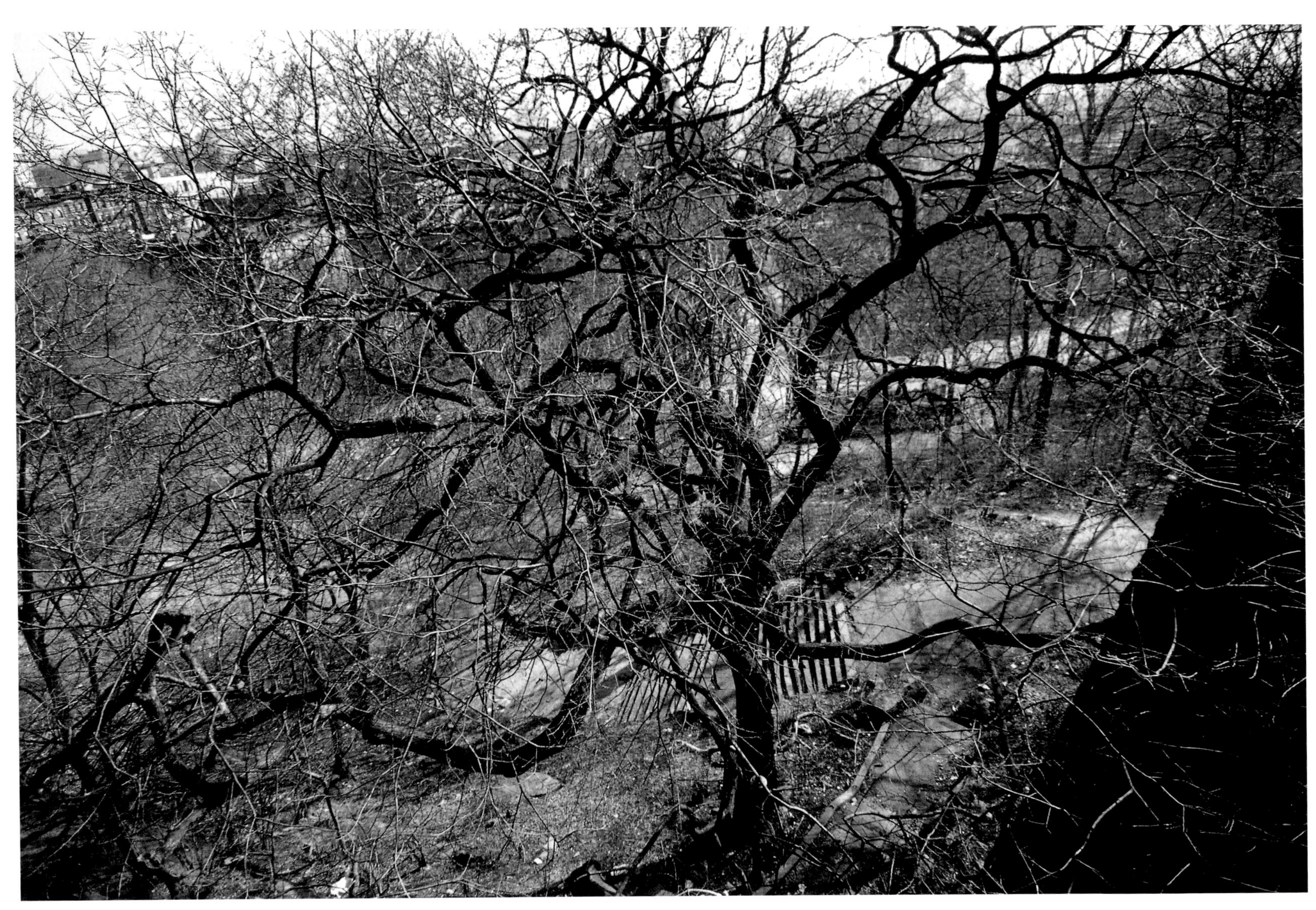

MORNINGSIDE PARK, 1990

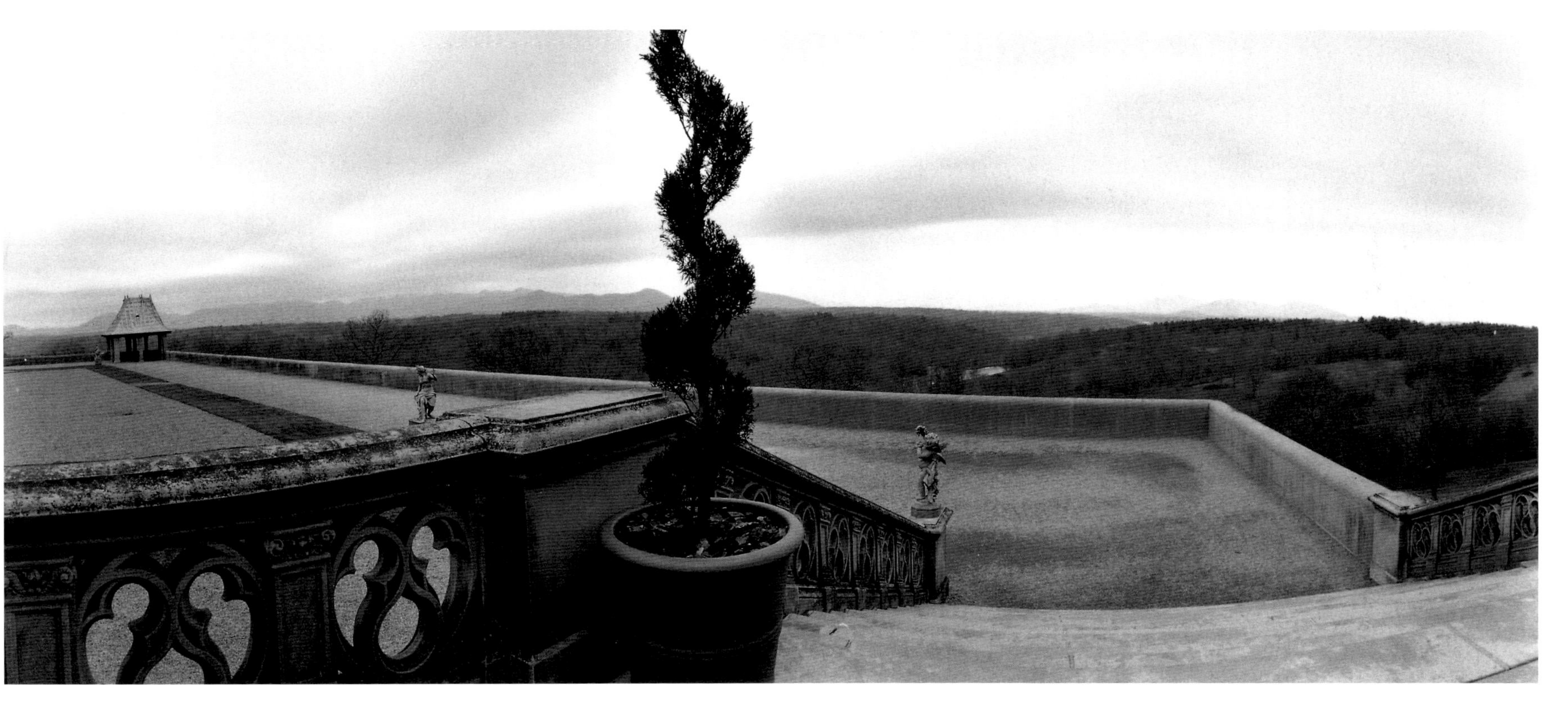

BILTMORE, 1994

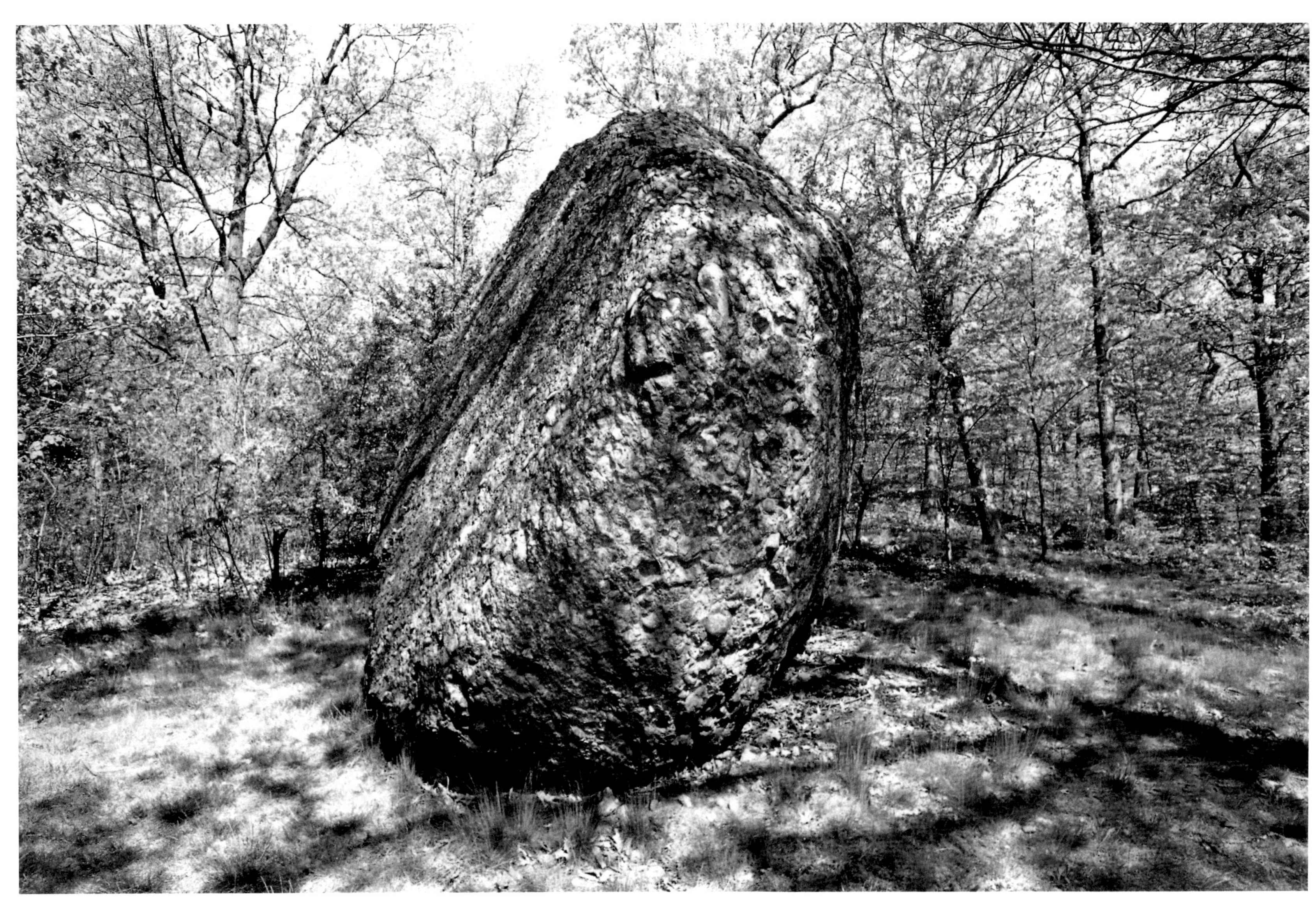

FRANKLIN PARK, 1991

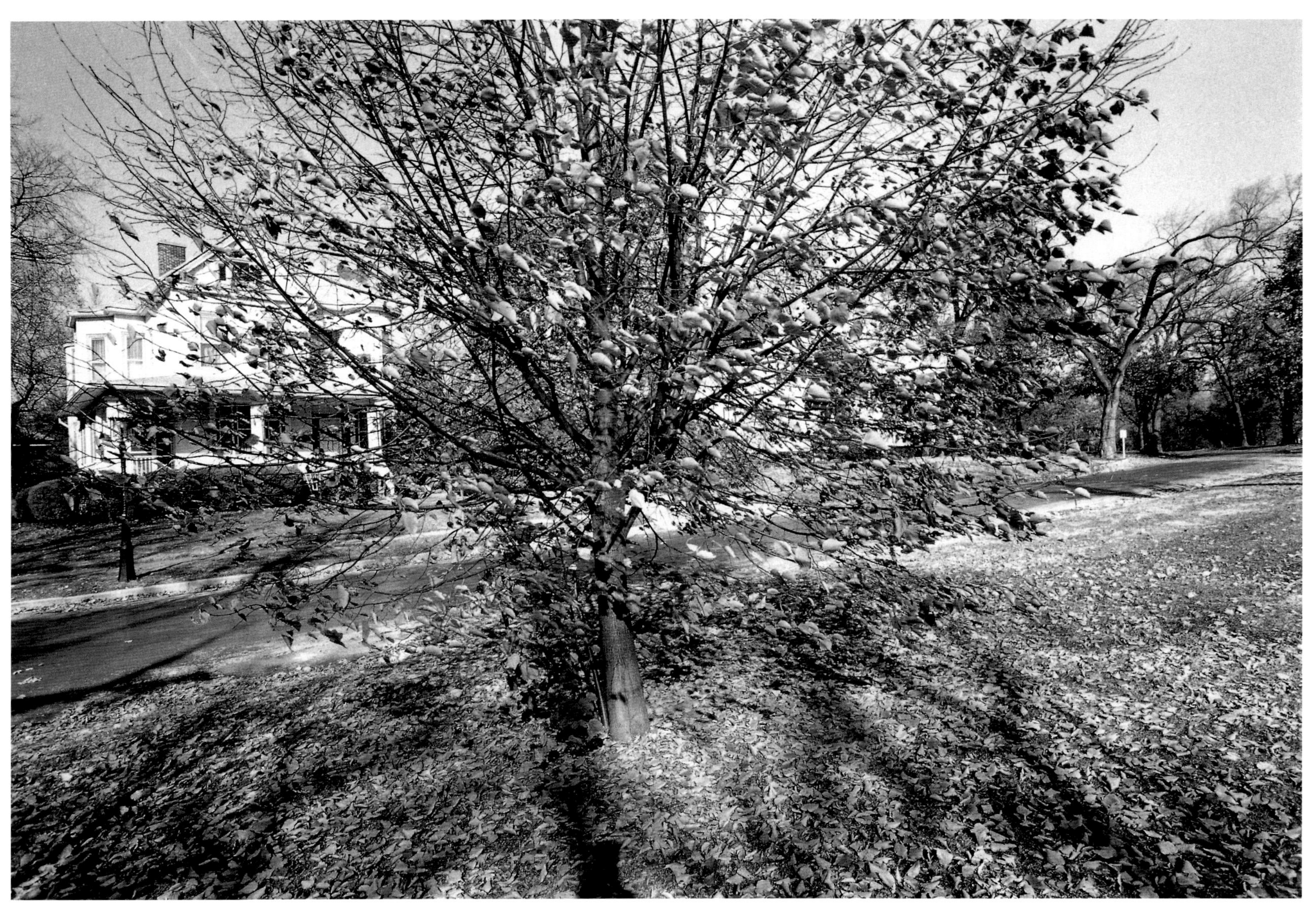

RIVERSIDE, 1988

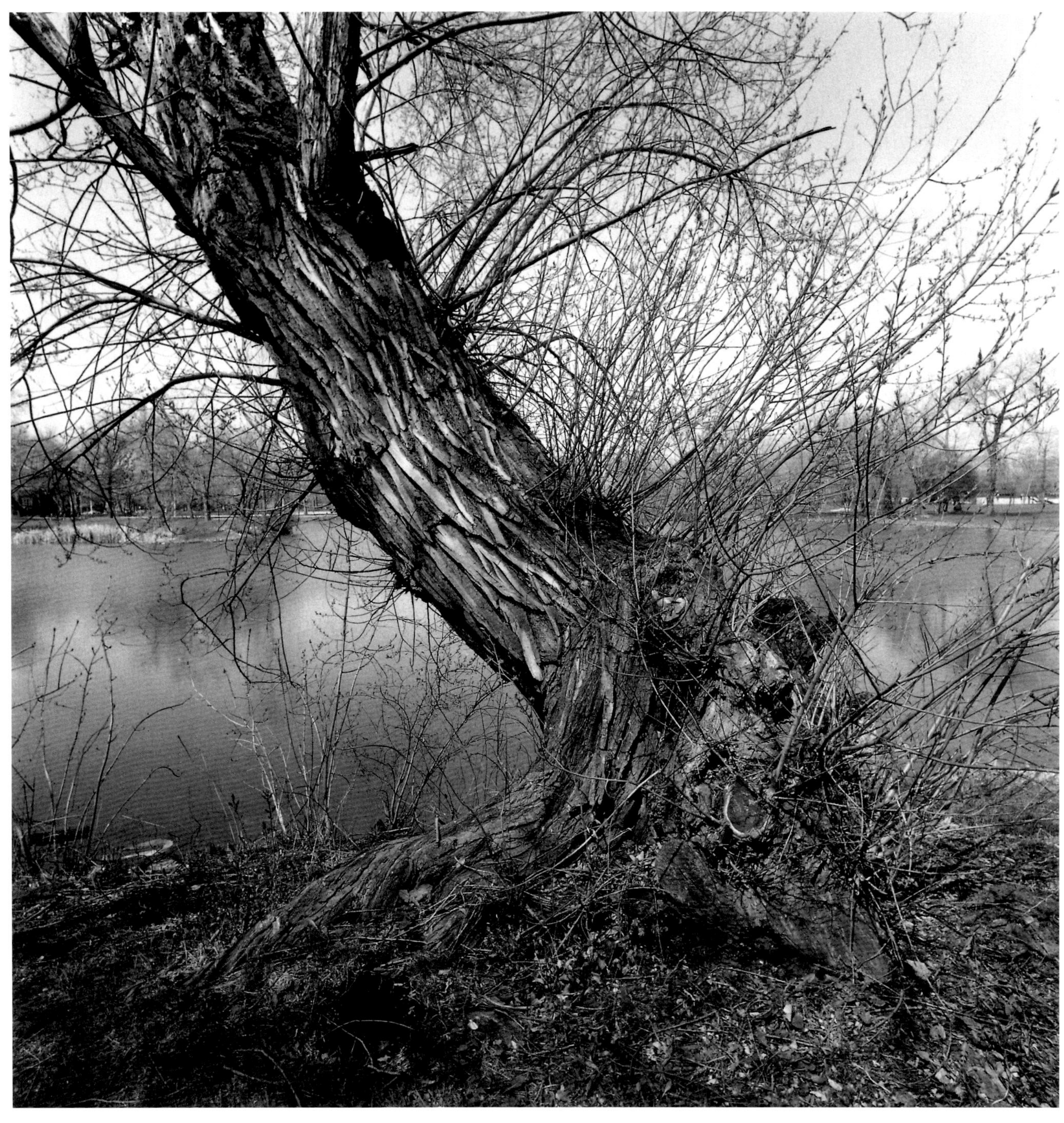

WASHINGTON PARK, 1992

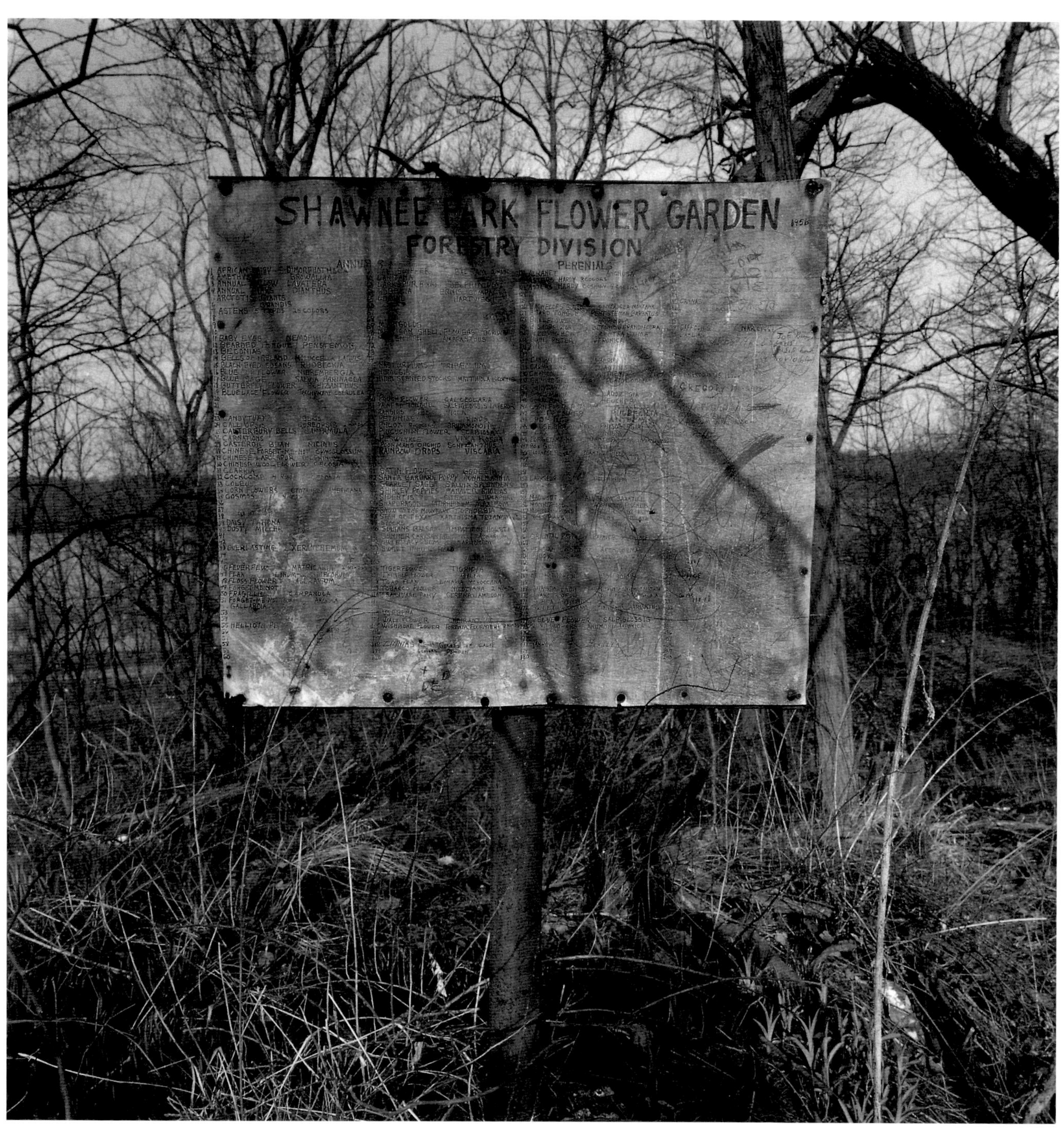

SHAWNEE PARK, 1994

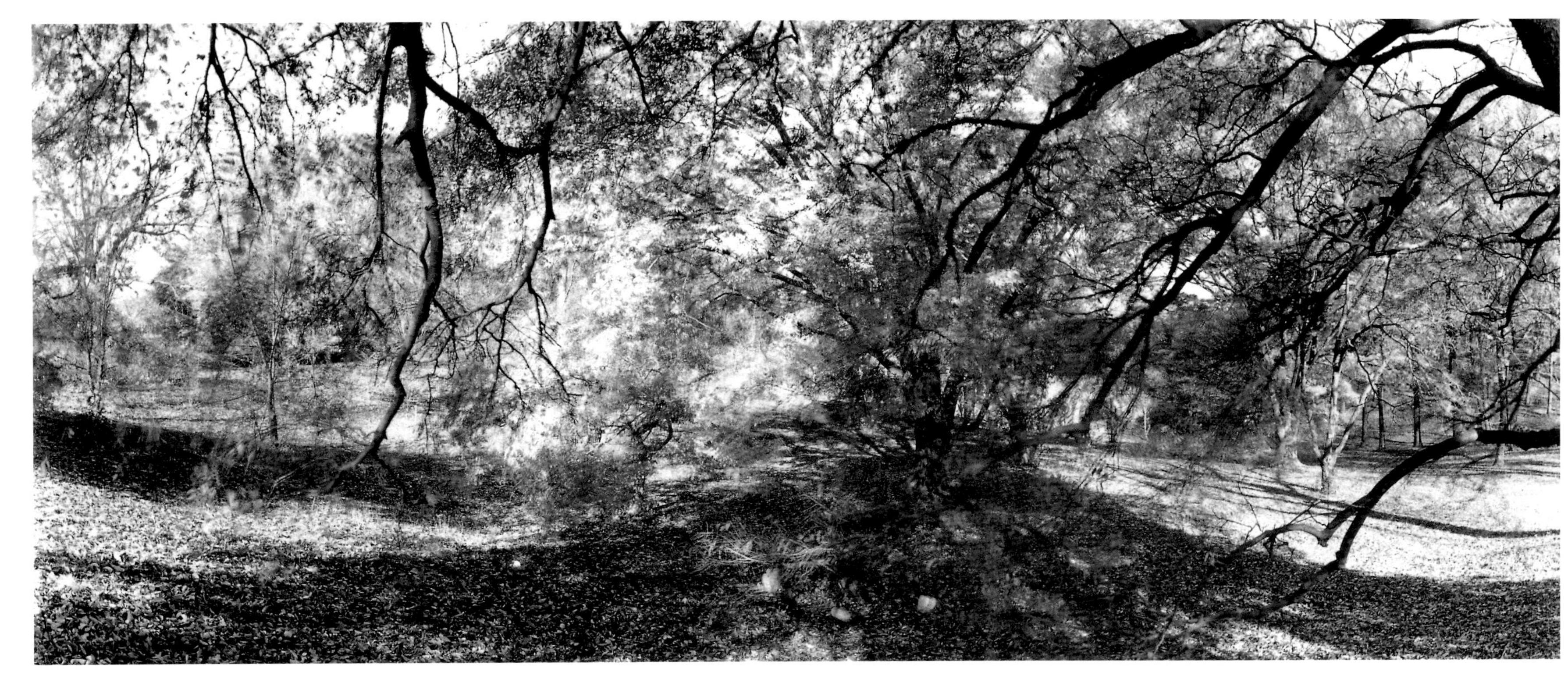

ARNOLD ARBORETUM, 1993

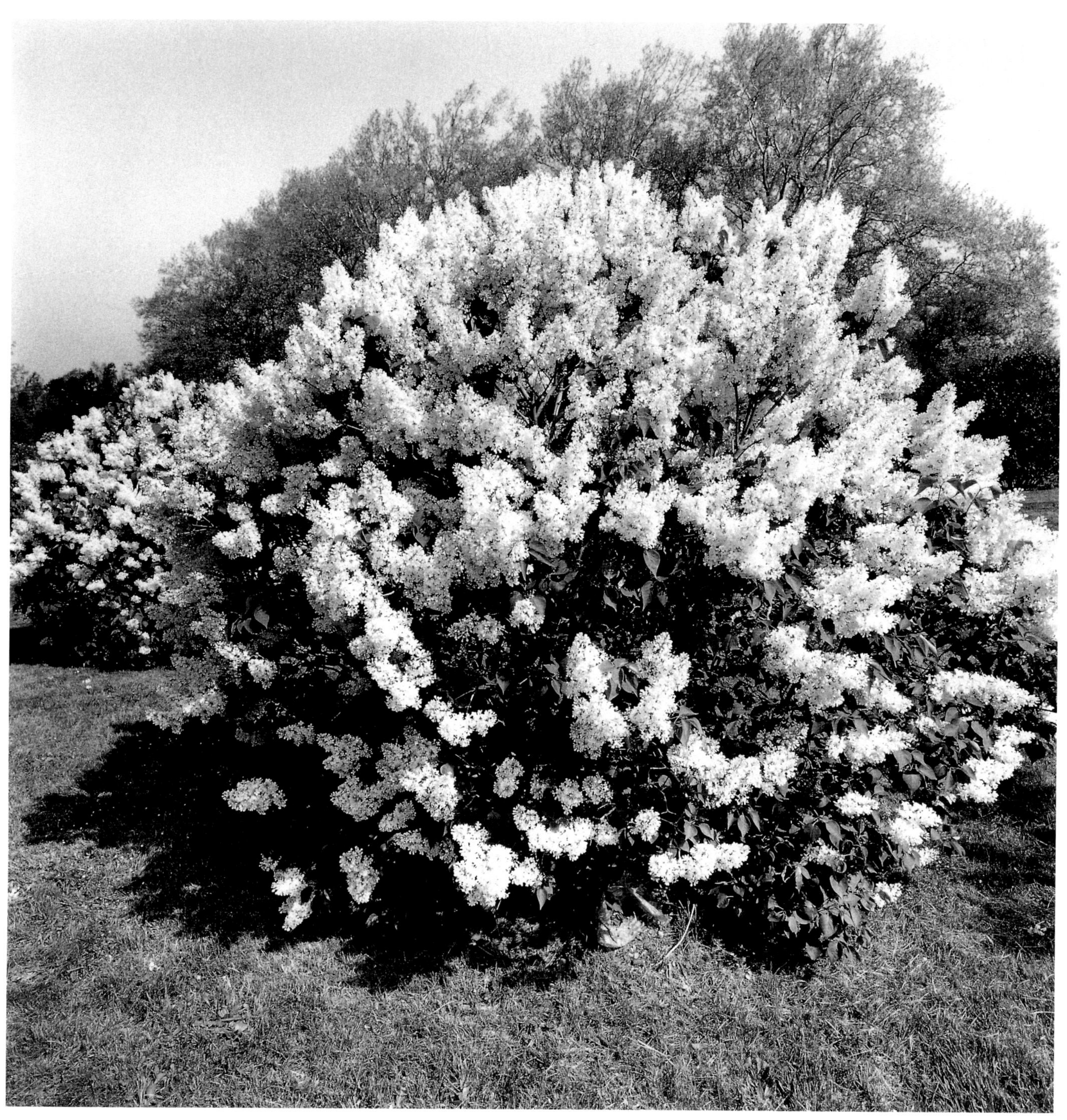

HIGHLAND PARK, 1993

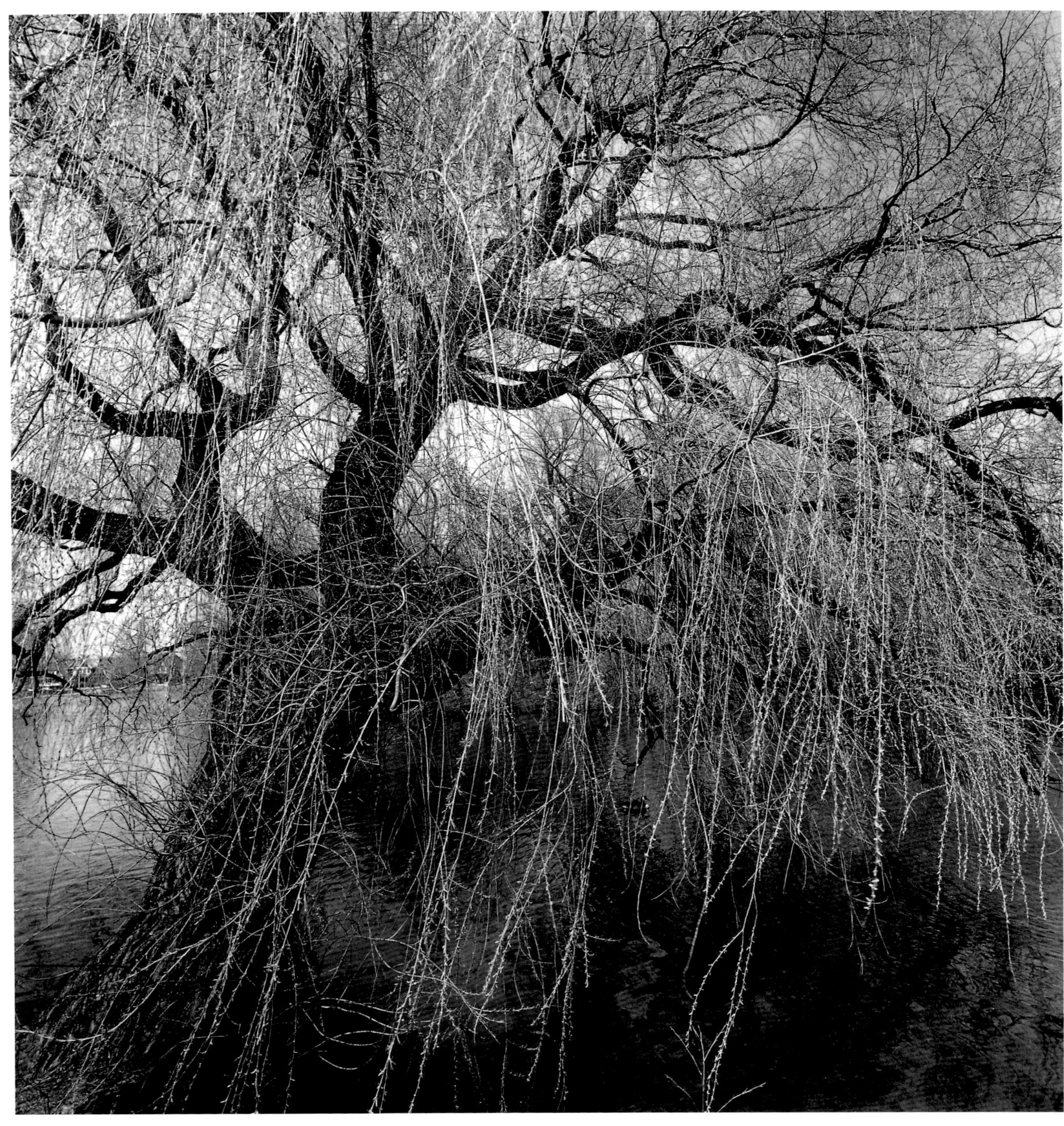

WASHINGTON PARK, 1992

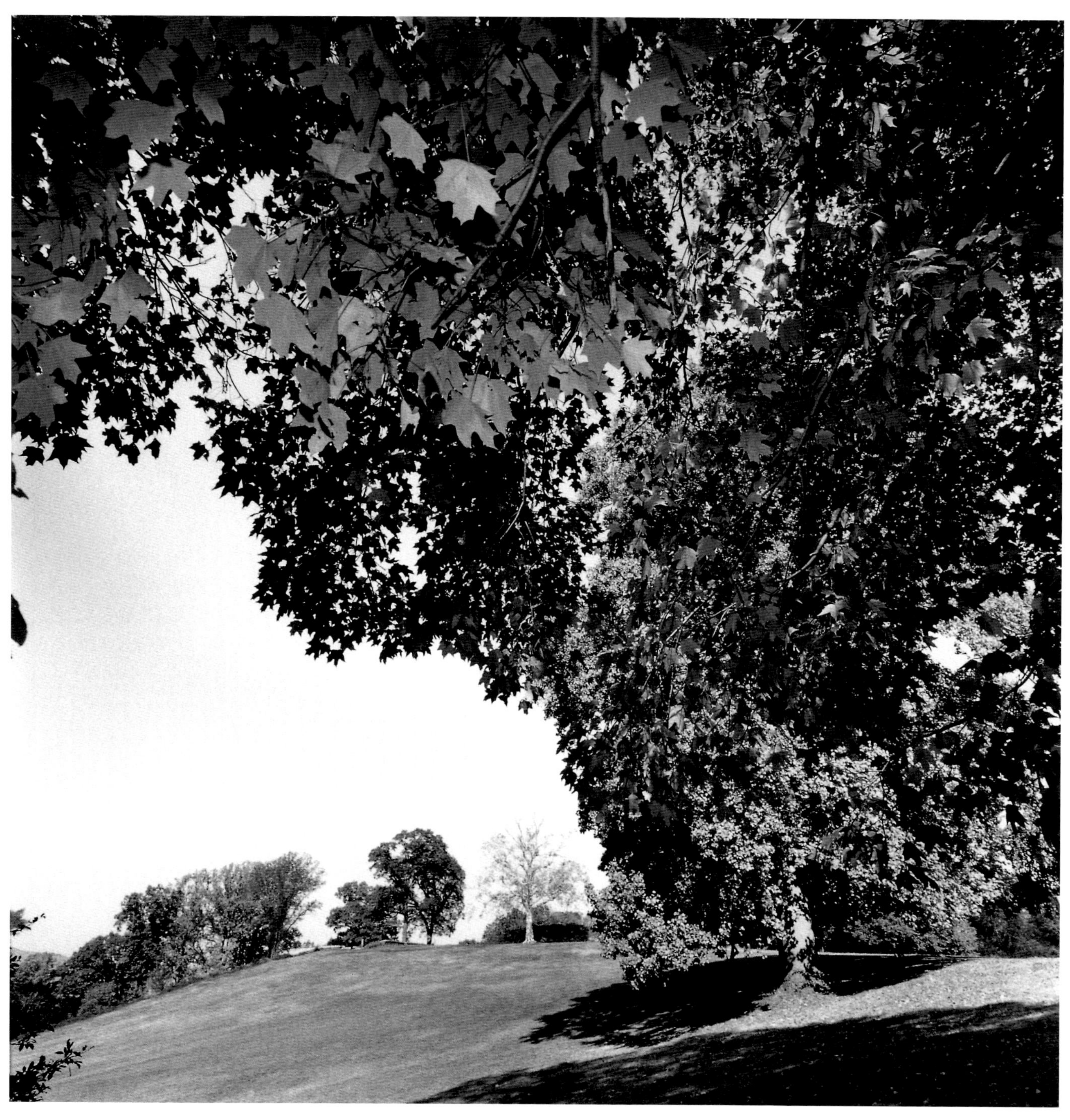

ROCKWOOD HALL, 1992

INTERVIEW WITH GEOFFREY JAMES

EDITED FROM AN INTERVIEW CONDUCTED BY DAVID HARRIS 23 JUNE 1995

I think most of the things I do begin with a kind of idle, relatively uninformed curiosity. I got interested in Olmsted partly through reading Robert Smithson's essay "Frederick Law Olmsted and the Dialectical Landscape" [*Artforum*, February 1973]. I guess what interested me in the idea of doing the project was that Olmsted was to me a mythical figure. There was quite a bit of writing on him, sort of an Olmsted scholarly industry, but nothing that visually described his œuvre now. It seemed to be a worthwhile thing to investigate.

Olmsted is central to North America, or to certain periods of it. I think he's probably not central now, but we'll get to that. There was an incredible energy in the building of these parks, an energy, a will to have them, which doesn't exist anymore. And some of the means to do it, which also probably don't exist anymore because the cities are too developed. The parks occurred at an absolutely strategic moment, and they were very important.

I've always been drawn to special places. I grew up near Avebury and Stonehenge and found them absolutely extraordinary. When I was in Italy, after doing the Italian gardens, photographing the Campagna, I became very interested in the Etruscan sites. These are essentially sacred places, the Etruscan sites and Avebury. What's interesting about them is that they have several characteristics in common. They're sited so that they command views all around, and they are defensible. They often have water, not the prehistoric British sites, but certainly the Etruscan sites – they have rivers and ravines. In a curious way, I think there are parts of the Olmsted parks that have similar characteristics. Scarborough Pond in Franklin Park, which is somewhat post-Olmsted, is very much part of the spirit of the place. It is a spot that provides many views. You can be in that area and see things coming from all directions. It is a very interesting, very complex site.

My Italian [gardens] project came out of a marriage between this absurdly inefficient machine [a 1920 Kodak panoramic camera] that had fallen into my hands almost by accident in the late seventies. It seemed to be a different way of making pictures, something that I had instinctively felt I could use, especially in very confined spaces. Italian gardens are usually quite small. Small and complex, with multiple vistas. And it seemed to be very fruitful; the subject was fruitful in relation to the machine. I got wedded somehow to this machine, and it now seems incredible that it was basically all I had. I had only this two-hundred-dollar camera. All I did was walk around with this machine. It was very inefficient. You can take only about ten pictures a day working flat out. And you also lost a lot because it was a camera that effectively had no exposure controls at all. Very, very primitive, like the birth of photography.

This particular camera had no viewfinder. It had a scanning lens. It had a flip-up frame that was very approximate, and nails on the top that were like rifle sights, which gave you a fairly precise idea of the end of the scan so the vertical cut could be established. The horizontal cut you had to intuit basically; it was completely imprecise. The way you worked with this camera was very physical, you more or less photographed with your body. You had to put your body in a position where things felt very physical. You're there, the machine sees everything sharp – you don't – but you're there. I wanted to make pictures that had some balance in them, without being in any way symmetrical, which I dislike because it's too static. The funny thing about a panoramic camera is that it's actually not very good at panoramas. If you take panoramic views they're incredibly dull. I learned how to deal with foreground, background, with multiple viewpoints, different scales and levels of complexity and also how to make the picture work on a curved plane because the image is being made on a curved plane. It is quite different. You cannot see it, but you know it is curved and then it is going to be straightened out. But you never see that; you cannot see that when you are taking the pictures. You have to intuit what the picture would be scrolled out. All of this to say that I worked for ten years with such a crude machine and what I learned was how to make pictures that worked intuitively without worrying too much about the edge.

That machine worked in certain situations, did not work in others. And then, working on the parks, I got the 8 x 10. The wonderful thing about the 8 x 10, as I learned how to use it, is that it allows you to make pictures that place you there. The surfaces of the world are described in a very beautiful way. The panoramic camera lends itself to a certain austerity. It is very austere in its description, whereas the 8 x 10 has a plenitude and generosity about it, which I have learned to love.

When I started to work with the 8 x 10, I had only one lens, a 10¾-inch lens, which was not very wide. It was very close to a normal lens. I found it very constricting, that I couldn't get enough in; it was too simple. As the years went by I got wider and wider lenses until I ended up with something like the equivalent of a 25 or 28 mm on a 35 mm camera. That would be the lens I would put on in the morning and very rarely take off.

As I started using wider and wider lenses, it became much more interesting for me to photograph, because there would be a possible complexity. I learned that before you can make a picture, you have to find the spot, and you find the spot by walking. There is a walking activity with the machine and you are not peering through it – you are sort of sniffing, you are like a dog, trying to find the right spot. It is very, very instinctive. There were certain places that seemed to me had been designed, were consciously designed, to make you do this walk, to move your body through the space. There is always a sense of anticipation and richness of something to come – a journey to be made, almost a narrative. Sometimes I thought I could deal with it, other times I could not.

When I worked with the panoramic camera, I ended up sitting on the ground with this ridiculous black bag, putting the camera in and as I was doing this, I'd be looking around. It would take about ten minutes; then I'd see another picture. And that, in a way, is how I learned about that. You know if the space is good and you stay there for five, ten minutes, you'll see something else. You are sitting there on the ground with this thing and suddenly you've got a new viewpoint that looks interesting. That process was really good. Even with the 8 x 10, you have to set it up; it's not done instantly. You're in one spot and you're inhabiting that spot, and, all of a sudden, you see other possibilities. Which happens much more with a 35 mm. You see it on a 35 mm, you're moving up to the spot, moving constantly, and clicking. It's a different process, a process of endless refinement.

The modern panoramic camera is much wider. It has a much wider lens so that the vertical bite is bigger, and horizontally it gives 145 degrees as opposed to 120 degrees. It was quite difficult to work with it at the beginning because it was so inclusive: you're dealing with a lot more information. Again it's very physical and I think it's absolutely useless for panoramas. I think you really have to be in there with it. I always thought of the panoramas in particular as being fictions. They put together elements that the eye doesn't normally do. I think it's very hard to make a picture of a tree, of just one or two trees in the middle of nowhere. In a way, I think that the 8 x 10 allows you to do this because it renders so much information. Sometimes it allows you to make very, very simple pictures that you couldn't do with another apparatus.

I took very few vertical pictures. In fact I ended up working with an 8 x 10 camera that has no real vertical capacity. I was almost condemned to making horizontal pictures. Again, the tree forms are absolutely central. There is a kind of drawing. When you're making the picture, you're never articulating anything, you're working on a totally nonverbal level and responding to the space. It's a further exploration.

You move, you walk, and your body tells you what to take, where to take the picture. It's not really your eye. Now you find a spot in which you have a relationship to something around you, and the relationship immediately is interesting, and you put your camera down and you make a picture. You obviously can't put a view camera to your eyes as you walk around. This is one of the nice things. There's nothing to look through; I don't have a viewfinder. I guess these things imprint themselves, sometimes almost subconsciously, that there's something interesting there, that this line of trees is interesting. It's a way of dealing with the space. In a sense, the spaces themselves are designed to want to make you move forward. So I'm attracted when not everything is revealed. There is a sense of anticipation: you want to walk over that hill and see what's there.

I don't think it could be stressed too much, that there is almost no subject when you're photographing Olmsted. There is a subject, but the subject is the conditions of light. They change and the places change completely from one season to the next. Different pictures appear; the places could never be fully represented. To that extent, they resemble cities. You could never "image" a city in its totality because everyone has a circuit through it. You have your circuit, you have certain places you go, certain places you always walk, other places you've never walked at all because you're not really interested. Same thing with a park. You find a circuit that in a deep animal way appeals to you. I tend to go back to the same places. I would look at everything, but there would be whole areas of Franklin, for example, that I just found very uninteresting. The wooded areas, in particular, which were in very bad shape and really sad in a way. Areas that I think Lee was always drawn to; he was drawn to the woods just across from the country meadow, walks that are shabby, run-down, not much landscaped.

I think one could have done a wonderful project just on one park. Both Prospect and Franklin could have sustained a three- or four-year absolutely minute investigation. If I had the means, I'd probably keep going, maybe just in one or two parks. I read the other day Robert Adams quoting Dorothea Lange that most photographers leave the subject too quickly; they think they've taken all of the pictures that ought to be taken. If you keep on, you could actually keep trying new things. I think it's absolutely true. The good places are very hard to exhaust. Look at Atget.

My response to Prospect Park in Brooklyn, to the Long Meadow, was almost identical to Tony Hiss's description in his article "Experiencing Places" [*New Yorker*, 22 June 1987], a piece about spaces. When you start at the Endale Arch and you enter the Meadow you are inexorably led on. The grading is brilliant and you're led on until – he doesn't talk about this – but I think there is a point about two-thirds of the way through the walk when suddenly it's pay-off time, because you can look in both directions: you can see where you are going to get to and you can see where you have come from. It's a spectacular space.

There is another part of Prospect Park where I never get the picture I wanted – the transition from Nethermead to the Lake. There's a sort of walkway, when you're walking past the Great Lookout, and in either direction it is brilliant. If you approach Nethermead from the Lake, you go up and you know there is this great space beyond, but it is not revealed until the last minute. Similarly, when you are in the Nethermead, you know there is an exit and the Lake. It is an astonishing piece of grading and it's very deliberate, very subtle, and, for me, impossible to convey photographically. I tried all manners and ways to take it, but it never worked. I couldn't do it.

One year, I made photographs in February on a very cold winter day. I've never been so cold in my life. Prospect Park was deserted. It was very bright, clear light and I was in an interesting mood. One thing I have learned, and it's illustrated in the *Campagna* book, where there are two pictures of the aqueduct Claudia, made within ten minutes of each other on either side of a gate. One is shot into the sun and the other has the sun behind me. You come back to the conditions of light. Whichever way you face, the picture changes completely. I was fascinated by this. It's totally different. It's the same day, but completely different pictures.

I think that these spaces are tragically empty and underused, that they speak of some kind of breakdown. There are always efforts to resuscitate them; sometimes they are quite impressive and wonderful. Central Park is the exception. There are 40 million visits a year – it works. Prospect is still moot. By that time I had seen a lot of the spaces and you realize that they are all in the same shape, that they are monuments to the breakdown of something.

I don't know whether I realized at the beginning how moralizing the Olmsted spaces were, how improving they were, that they were supposed to improve people not just physically but also morally. That the contemplation of this sort of landscape would make you a better person. It would refine your taste, and allow you to go back fit for work on Monday. All that seems a bit quaint and dated, and I suspect it was obsolete even in his time.

When you're there, no one can believe that what you're photographing is the park. "You're photographing the hawks?" Or, as someone asked, "Are you doing a puzzle?" This huge jigsaw puzzle. That's the closest they ever got. Yes, I'm doing a jigsaw puzzle. But the notion that the space itself might be of interest. . . . Very few people realize now that the spaces were really created; most people think that they were just a parcel of nature fenced off.

To me, the function of a photographer, or one of the functions of a photographer, is to point things out. If you have the luxury of being able to think about things and to work as we have on this project, to work slowly and over the years, and to learn about them, it's a chance to show something that people haven't thought about that much. I don't have a huge didactic ambition, but everything I've done is an attempt to convey my sense of excitement about these creations. And not just to illustrate them, but to give a sense of what it's like to be there. Which is what the best photography does. It's like being there; it has a mnemonic power that no other medium has. A power to recall things, which painting doesn't have. You can look at an Impressionist painting, and it's a beautiful thing, but you're not there. You're too aware of the paint. And the medium is so apparent. The medium takes over; you see Impressionist painting. In photography, you see that seamless surface. I'm not saying anything new, but I think it's harder than it appears actually to make pictures that have this existential weight. The good people do it, like Walker Evans. The good people put you right there.

I suppose the real subject of the parks is their persistence. At the heart of most of these places, the sheer strength of Olmsted's vision and abilities persists. The places have persisted, whatever shape they are in. They haven't been turned into shopping malls yet; maybe into golf courses, but they are still there. There's a kind of persistence, and within them – and possibly in my pictures – there are hints of what might have been. On certain beautiful mornings when the light is clean, they are exquisite places to be. And you have them to yourself. The places are the sum total of an incredible amount of energy.

INTERVIEW WITH ROBERT BURLEY

EDITED FROM AN INTERVIEW CONDUCTED BY DAVID HARRIS 30 JUNE 1995

I think one of the important lessons of that first trip to the Olmsted park system in Boston in 1988 was that these sites were overwhelming. They were huge – spaces you could spend days walking through and still have missed very important parts. They were places that changed not only on a season-to-season basis, but week to week, even day to day. Often, I would find after having visited one place and gone back a few days later, there would be some change in the foliage or the activity that made it quite a different place from the first time I visited. So it was in many ways an ongoing and never-ending search for not only good pictures, but a search for an overview of these particular sites.

I saw myself as someone trying to record an essence of a place, to try to get at some deeper quality or feeling of what a place was like to be in. When you're trying to achieve this, really all you can rely on is your own personal experience and how your past experience relates to the situation and place you're in at the time.

I was constantly trying to place timeless elements next to those that were in flux. And to make a suggestion of an infrastructure that stayed put next to a landscape that was changing on a day-to-day basis and the activity of people who were changing on a minute-to-minute basis. So the element of time is a subtle undercurrent that I tried quite hard to produce. But it is a very definite undercurrent in the work.

This is a picture of Central Park in 1990, on the upper west side of the park. It was done in January on an overcast day, near the beginning of the project, so it's one of those days where I dragged myself out thinking, "I'm not going to get anything, the light's no good." I did a number of pictures and thought, "I doubt if any of them are going to be keepers." But when I made a print, I was pleasantly surprised by its wonderful, rather limited palette, its richness: the greys of the stonework and the asphalt path, the browns and yellows in the dead leaves that cover the ground. I was excited by how very much this is a colour photograph. The colour is a kind of subtext to the image; it's rather incidental. I realized these were the kinds of days that I could use to just look at the places. The colour was always part of the place but never the main reason for making the photograph.

Often people have spoken to me about this and said, "Why don't you photograph when the landscapes are at their most colourful?" – thinking that would be in the summer months. But I found that the landscapes were at their most colourful in the fall and spring. In the fall, you get an incredible range of reds and browns and yellows, just after everything's died off. I found the fall colour a little too overwhelming, which I avoided with the exception of one or two trips, simply because I felt that the colour overtook the photographs. In the spring, as things were greening, there were a thousand and one different colours of green. The trees were open; you could see through them. It's also a time of year when the landscapes are very active, things are changing very quickly, the places are undergoing a kind of rebirth. Colour adds that dimension of time. It also adds the dimension of pure pleasure that we experience when we're in these places: colour is certainly a very important part of such pleasure. But in the summer things fill out and a monotonous forest green takes over. You're really stuck with one colour, with this very limited palette. The couple of trips when I did try to photograph in the summer I found very disappointing and not very successful.

By 1992 I'd gathered up enough courage to go and do fall colour. One of the things I was worried about was that I'd just end up with a bunch of calendar pictures. By calendar pictures I mean photographs that are strictly about the beauty of fall colours. They just end up being too picturesque in a very traditional sense. They end up being too pretty, too seductive; you can't get beyond the colour of the image to the place itself. This was a photograph done at Ward's Pond, a place in the Emerald Necklace that I have always been quite attracted to and am very fond of – I always end up there when I go to Boston. I had a nice, soft, overcast day and I deliberately went just as the fall colour was dying out. I didn't go at its height; I went just as things are ready to drop off the trees. I was there for two weeks, and the first week I had fall colour with the leaves on the trees. By the end of the second week, the trees were bare. That tells you how quickly things change. But the colour in this picture is just restrained enough for you to appreciate that time of the year.

It's not about looking at those trees at that time of the year, it's more about people looking at those trees at that time of the year. In a way, it's a comment on the kind of picture that's so easy to create in the fall. What makes it an interesting picture as well as a successful picture is the inclusion of two small figures, surrounded on all sides by rich colour, and the feeling of nature. If Olmsted had put "X"s on his plans to indicate vistas to the park visitors, I think they would be standing on one.

One of the surprising things about these spaces, which are public parks, public spaces, is that they're wonderful spaces to go to be alone. Even though they're very public and open, they're wonderful places to be by yourself and contemplate things and just clear your head. Certainly, one of the real pleasures of this whole project was that through the process of photographing, I enjoyed a luxurious situation where I could wander through the parks and partake in that activity.

I know photographers who use view cameras have the reputation for being very patient. People who use this camera system are known to set up their camera and wait for the light, the people, or whatever to all come together. Even though I use the view camera almost exclusively, I'm actually very impatient. The way I work is, if I see something about to happen, or if I see something starting to happen, I'll set my camera up, and I get quite involved and excited by the prospect of having to get the camera set up, get everything in focus, get the film into the back of the camera, and get the shot before it disappears. It's like a drawn-out decisive moment. It's a decisive moment with a view camera.

I felt that especially places like Central Park had not only a very deep history in a public sense, but a very deep history for a lot of the people who have used them over the years. It was a feeling I've always had walking through Central Park. You wonder about the millions of people who have used that park over the years and all the day-to-day rituals that have taken place over and over again. One of the photographs to suggest that idea is one photograph at the Ladies' Pavilion, by the lake, with a rock formation. In it are two lovers who were aware of me bumbling away over by the Pavilion. With my equipment, my tripod, and my view camera. I wasn't inconspicuous. I couldn't steal photographs with my subjects unawares. I think they felt I wasn't really including them in the photograph and if they did, they didn't care: they were necking and having a wonderful time, so it didn't matter. But near the lovers on the rock and just below them, on the rock formation, there's all sorts of graffiti, all sorts of personal notes about so-and-so loving so-and-so, and little love poems.

You're trying to make pictures; you're caught up in all the logistics of trying to catch these figures somehow in a relationship to all these other elements: the rock formation, the decorative ironwork of the Ladies' Pavilion, the spring trees in the background, the lake. I didn't even notice the graffiti on the rocks until after I enlarged the image. I didn't notice it while I was there. But once I had worked away in the darkroom and made a final print of this particular image, I was very pleased with it. It really did suggest that this is where love has taken place over and over again, that somehow this place lends itself to this very spiritual activity. These kinds of pictures were very difficult to come by; they were few and far between.

The homeless are these days very much a part of the American city, and one of the obvious places for them to live is in the public parks. When I was first working on the project, I did what everyone else did, I tried to pretend they weren't there. But as the project went on, of course, I would see the temporary shelters that they built and I would often meet them as well. They were people who actually lived in these parks, who knew them very well, and who were very much a part of them. And conversely the places were very much a part of their lives. They were their homes.

The purpose of bridges in Central Park is to connect one upper level with another. Not to take the point too far, but it suggests that two levels are always part of Central Park. These are two people who are out early in the morning, using the bridge to stretch their leg muscles and get ready for a run. They're up on the bridge and dressed in all their fancy jogging gear and expensive running shoes, and below the bridge is a man who slept under the bridge every night. In fact, what he would do – I noticed this either the day before or the next day – is he would get up at around eight-thirty, roll up his futon and leave it there, and then come back at night and unroll it and sleep. That was his place.

I've developed a strong respect for Olmsted. As a result of being able to return to a number of parks over a period of years, I found that they were constantly reinvented places, not just through the change of seasons and the different activities that took place there, but through Olmsted's design skills. He was someone who really had an immense talent for manipulating not only the landscape but the way people experienced it. Being a picture-maker, one tries to be aware of how people view your pictures and how you can manipulate their eye around an image. Olmsted, as someone who created landscapes, was incredibly successful at manipulating me in a very deliberate way around his landscapes. Even when I was very much aware of it, and even when I tried to find alternative routes, I found myself following a kind of itinerary that I think he had probably developed. This was one of the most interesting realizations about these parks: how they were not designed just as beautiful places, they were designed very carefully to be experienced in a very deliberate manner. That's an amazing thing to be able to do, especially considering the scale and complexity of most of them. They're not backyards; these places consist of acres and acres of land. In the beginning I assumed there were probably areas he concentrated on more than others, but it was always the whole place. It was always from one edge of the park to the other.

INTERVIEW WITH LEE FRIEDLANDER

EDITED FROM AN INTERVIEW CONDUCTED BY DAVID HARRIS 6 JUNE 1995

I like commissions generally. I have also turned down commissions that did not interest me. The Olmsted one is peculiar in that it came at the same time that I had become personally interested in landscapes. It was perfect timing. Usually you end up using what you know rather than discovering all the time, whereas in this project it was more of a discovering experience because I was and am now trying to learn about landscapes. Plus the project occurred in places that often resembled natural landscapes. Obviously Central Park resembles the city too, not just the woods. Let's drop the word commission and say that with the material, one could spend six years or a lifetime at it. There is no real end point; if you were crazed enough with Olmsted or parks, you could really just keep going forever. I love them because they have perimeters and you are stuck with what is inside of a box in a sense.

I hadn't a clue about anything on Olmsted. I figured, if what he did is worth its salt, it will be in the pictures, somewhere. I didn't think I needed to be a scholar, but give me the raw material and let me see what I can make with it. I also knew that Geoffrey was very involved with the idea; he always would try to tell me [facts about Olmsted], and I'd say, "Okay, Geoffrey; I'm glad to know that." But I just wanted to be let loose in these places and see what happened. I figure it's inevitable that if you moved as much dirt as Geoffrey once told me was done – it's got to be clear that something's there. I don't go with too many preconceptions of what's possible. In a sense you want to approach it with a certain kind of innocence. I do, that's my game.

I tend to like places that aren't flat. So I probably stayed away from those big fields and went toward the hilly parts or the parts with water. It just gives you some other games to play. I tend to like more than one thing in my pictures. I don't know why, but it's one of the pleasures I get out of doing it.

I think the hardest places were the subdivisions. It's hard to know what to do with them. . . . I think that Riverside is probably one of the better shapes of a suburb; it also had a big park on a river, so it was very pretty. There was lots to do there. The ones in Boston were more city-like and there was one in Atlanta – Druid Hills. It was very nice but it was more of a landscape city, whereas Riverside had a big park abutting the river.

The places are interesting in most cases, but not every one. For instance, Louisville has three parks and the one that interested me the most was Shawnee. I don't even know why. Cherokee is obviously a nicer, bigger, better-kept park, which Geoffrey liked the best of those three. In the third one, Iroquois, it was very hard to find vantage points or even see. There wasn't any place to park and they made it inaccessible to the public. So I'm not sure why one likes one better than another, but I had a good time in Cherokee too.

I just always knew there was more to do in World's End even though I went two or three times. But you realize that there is something about World's End and you just keep going back to it for a long time. It's hard not to like Central Park or Prospect; they are special too.

The set of five photographs from Jackson Park – that building [the Museum of Science and Industry] and the trees – it's funny how they almost work like one picture. They come together; there's something nice about those together. I was surprised that Phyllis felt the same way when she saw them. It's something I've never been able to get anybody to do, even in an installation: to put groups together. Because I work so much, often there are things that would look wonderful – nine in a square or twelve in a close group – but I hardly ever get the opportunity to have that done.

The reason I started using [the Hasselblad superwide] was that I was having some kind of congenital problem with wide-angle lenses [on the Leica] in the desert, probably because of the light, and probably because those lenses were designed for flat surfaces. Those lenses are usually used by people who do architectural work, which deals with flat surfaces, not so much with a large area with lots of details. I don't know what the reasons were. It looked as if areas were out of focus and they wouldn't be the same every time. I call it congenital because it comes with the lens; it's not something anybody can fix and it's not that anybody even knows why. I've talked to technical people and they don't know. So every time I saw a photographer who I knew was good technically, like Frank Gohlke, I would ask, "Hey, Frank, what's the best wide-angle lens you know of?" The common denominator was the Hasselblad superwide. The Hasselblad superwide is really a very primitive piece of equipment. It's probably been around since I was fifteen or sixteen years old. They've improved the basic design, but it's really a fancy box camera: it has no rangefinder, it has no meter. Considering what cameras are made of these days, it's just a box, it's a lens on a back. I didn't want to change gear, sizes, enlargers, the whole thing, but reluctantly I went and bought it and then I fell in love with it. It was a relief after thirty years to have a different shape to deal with, and the lens didn't have any problems in the desert.

When I first started walking with it [the Hasselblad] in the parks along with the Leica, I didn't know which one to use: the tried and true, which I knew, or the one I was trying to learn how to use. So finally I just said, "I can't take the Leica. I'll just have to leave it at home or I'll never learn how to use this camera." It's schizophrenic, so I just used it and still am using it a lot.

One's square [the Hasselblad] and one's rectangular [the Leica], and you have to just get used to using it, that's all. It's like getting in one car or another, I suppose. With the square – this is very personal – it seemed to me that I was able to get more sky, which I've always wanted. It seemed to be the same rectangle with more sky on top. And it still feels that way. It's the same stuff that you get, but you get more of the sky. I always wanted more sky out of a horizontal picture. All of a sudden the whole tree is in the picture.

Oh, panorama – it's the kind of camera I think I have always been fascinated with. All of a sudden somebody came out with one that looked like it was made well. In the past, they weren't made well and the lenses weren't very good. This one [Noblex] is just a very good little camera. So it came about at a time when I was playing with other things and I thought I might as well play with it. I like working with the panorama too.

None of my cameras has ground glass. That's a kind of freedom in itself; it's faster, as long as you understand what the perimeters are. With a bigger camera you see the perimeters when you look at the ground glass. I don't think the Leica is any different than any other camera with an optical viewfinder. At a certain distance from your head, a lot of things are going to take place. There could be errors and they could be errors to your advantage because you have to learn how to use them technically. I think the biggest difference, if the sun is out, is that I'd probably take four or five times as many pictures because I might not need a tripod. I can work much faster. I like sun; I'm just a fair-weather photographer. If I could have my druthers, bright, clear light would be my choice, mainly because I can just keep going. I usually develop the film pretty close to the time – within two weeks – of when I shot. I'm not in such a hurry for contacts and not at all in a hurry to look at them or to mark them up. With a project like this, after the first year I got farther behind because that's just the way my life is. Then toward the end I had to do a blitz of printing and it was really madness. I like to make a lot of rough prints, but I usually don't show them to many people. This project is unique because I really did my editing with all of you.

As far as I was concerned, Phyllis chose the best pictures, maybe with your help or with Geoffrey's or mine. I wasn't in the least bit anxious about that after the first year because she seemed like a kindred spirit of the pictures, so it was fun. It meant that I didn't have to do it all at home. And in a sense I got to see them better. Most of the time I wouldn't want to do that with somebody else, but I enjoyed doing it with all of you.

If you take somebody like Michael Jordan, and if you said to him, "Michael, at a certain point when you are running down the field and the ball comes to you, what are you going to do?" he would look at you as if you were crazy. Because there are a thousand things he could do: he could move almost anywhere or he could pass off or he could shoot or he could dribble. He wouldn't even have a clue because he would have to see what was happening. And I think that's very similar to photography, which I don't think is similar to painting or writing in most cases. That little tiny moment is a beginning and an end and it has something to do with the same kind of mentality that an athlete has to use. I was watching tennis, for example. The tricks that good tennis players use, especially what happens when the ball bounces and does odd things. You couldn't predict what you're going to do. He's going to serve to you; what are you going to do? Try to hit it back. Not only try to hit it back, try to hit it back in a weird way. Or in some articulate way. And I think photography is stuck with those same kinds of moments, especially if you're not a studio photographer. You don't have much control.

If the sun goes behind a cloud, the whole place looks different. You have to regroup in a sense. If the sun changes you have to regroup in all kinds of ways, exposure-wise, how you might develop it, you have to juggle things around technically. A great day is really one of those days where there are a few clouds because here you are looking at something and you could make two different pictures from the same standpoint within a minute because of the wonderful changes that happen. So it's not so unusual that you would go back to the same tree because it interests you. And because you're going to hit it at a different time, you might not even recognize it. When I work in the desert, which is even more remote, I'll have five pictures from five different years of the same cactus. And I don't even know it until I start to print. I just go there and every time it looms up as the interesting thing.

Sometimes working with a camera, somebody does something that's just beyond belief. Gary Winogrand takes pictures of things that in your wildest dreams you wouldn't think could exist in the world. There's a picture of a cow's tongue in a cowboy's hat that becomes a beautiful thing; it looks like a piece of architecture. In your wildest dreams you wouldn't come up with that and that's just because he was aware that it might be possible. He was there when it happened and his head worked that way. Or that couple on Fifth Avenue with the monkey that looks like a family. Nutty pictures, but the most imaginative person in the world would not come up with that set of things.

The question of where to stand is interesting. What we're really talking about is a vantage point. If you look at amateurs or people taking pictures, they do funny things. Most people obviously don't know where to stand. They're standing too close, they're contorted. They're humorous to watch, people who photograph, especially people who aren't in tune with their equipment, because they don't know when they pick it up what it will do. If you work with the same equipment for a long time, you get more in tune to what is possible. But within that there are still surprises. But using a camera day after day after day, within a framework, I'll do the same thing; I'll back up and I'll go forward with my body.

You don't have to be a fancy photographer to learn where to stand. Basically you're stuck with the frame and just like the person taking a picture of his family, who needs to go half a foot back – well, he doesn't step half a foot back – but on the other hand, he knows where to be if he hits it right. Now when you watch tennis you not only have the commentators, you also have the best of the old pros. You know how they repeatedly say, "Look at the way his back was formed when he took that shot." It really is important to them. They see that as a possibility of where the thing went. Probably the same thing is true of all of us.

You can pick at it, especially this project. I don't think anyone is capable of doing the definitive Central Park. In some ways we all – Bob and Geoffrey and myself – probably felt a relief, thinking, if I didn't get it somebody else did. Going out with those guys was fun because the ironies were just so hilarious. I could go out with them and you could almost have tied us so we were back to back, and one of us could be totally interested in one area and the other one the complete opposite. It was really funny that could happen. I don't think any of us who went out together were ever interested in the same thing. Very rare. Maybe a monument or some major object: I know there was a monument [the Maryland Monument] in Prospect I think we all photographed. That explains why I didn't need to read about Olmsted too.

LIST OF PHOTOGRAPHS IN THE PORTFOLIO

GEOFFREY JAMES

Unmounted gelatin silver prints

PAGE 29 "Southwood," the Barthold Schlesinger Estate, Brookline, Massachusetts, 1993. 13.6 x 33.3 cm. CCA PH1993:0426

30 The Long Meadow, Prospect Park, Brooklyn, New York, 1989. 8.5 x 26.5 cm. CCA PH1989:0163

31 The Boat House, Lullwater, Prospect Park, Brooklyn, New York, 1989. 8.6 x 26.6 cm. CCA PH1989:0164

32 Seaside Park, Bridgeport, Connecticut, 1991. 19.4 x 24 cm. CCA PH1992:0147

33 "Biltmore," the George W. Vanderbilt Estate, Asheville, North Carolina, 1990. 19.5 x 24.3 cm. CCA PH1991:0114

34 Cherokee Park, Louisville, Kentucky, 1993. 38.5 x 48.2 cm. CCA PH1995:0014

35 The Country Park, Franklin Park, Boston, Massachusetts, 1991. 19.5 x 24.4 cm. CCA PH1992:0267

36 "Rockwood Hall," the William D. Rockefeller Estate, Mount Pleasant (Tarrytown), New York, 1994. 19.5 x 24.5 cm. CCA PH1994:0073

37 The Country Park, Franklin Park, Boston, Massachusetts, 1991. 19.4 x 24.4 cm. CCA PH1992:0141

38 The Bridle Path Bridge, the Muddy River Improvement, Boston, Massachusetts, 1991. 18.2 x 24.6 cm. CCA PH1992:0136

39 The Meadowport Arch, Prospect Park, Brooklyn, New York, 1994. 19.5 x 24.1 cm. CCA PH1994:0065

40 The Vanderbilt Cemetery, Staten Island, New York, 1993. 19.3 x 24.5 cm. CCA PH1993:0410

41 The Bradbury Mausoleum, Mountain View Cemetery, Oakland, California, 1993. 13.5 x 33.9 cm. CCA PH1995:0035

42 The Cliff, Central Park, New York City, New York, 1994. 19.5 x 24.5 cm. CCA PH1994:0060

43 The Ramble, Central Park, New York City, New York, 1992. 19.5 x 24.5 cm. CCA PH1992:0111

44 The Wooded Island, Jackson Park, Chicago, Illinois, 1991. 19.6 x 24.6 cm. CCA PH1992:0129

45 The Country Park, Franklin Park, Boston, Massachusetts, 1994. 19.5 x 24.5 cm. CCA PH1994:0080

46 The Arnold Arboretum, Boston, Massachusetts, 1993. 19.3 x 23.2 cm. CCA PH1993:0422

47 The Arnold Arboretum, Boston, Massachusetts, 1994. 13.6 x 32.9 cm. CCA PH1994:0078

48 The Lake, Central Park, New York City, New York, 1991. 19.6 x 24.6 cm. CCA PH1992:0119

49 Mount Royal Park, Montréal, Québec, 1994. 13.5 x 32.6 cm. CCA PH1994:0086

Unmounted chromogenic colour prints

PAGE 51 Mount Royal Park, Montréal, Québec, 1990. 23.9 x 31.1 cm. CCA PH1991:0192

52 The Country Park, Franklin Park, Boston, Massachusetts, 1994. 35.7 x 45.7 cm. CCA PH1994:0031

53 The Country Park, Franklin Park, Boston, Massachusetts, 1994. 35.6 x 45.7 cm. CCA PH1994:0030

54 Point Chautauqua, near Buffalo, New York, 1994. 23.4 x 30.1 cm. CCA PH1994:0054

55 "Fairsted," the Frederick Law Olmsted residence and office, Brookline, Massachusetts, 1992. 24.2 x 31 cm. CCA PH1992:0240

56 The Herrick Memorial, Mountain View Cemetery, Oakland, California, 1991. 35.6 x 45.7 cm. CCA PH1992:0175

57 The Tennis House, the Long Meadow, Prospect Park, Brooklyn, New York, 1990. 35.4 x 45.6 cm. CCA PH1990:0291

58 The Bethesda Fountain, Central Park, New York City, New York, 1990. 35.4 x 45.5 cm. CCA PH1990:0265

59 "Rockwood Hall," the William D. Rockefeller Estate, Mount Pleasant (Tarrytown), New York, 1994. 35.7 x 45.7 cm. CCA PH1994:0047

60 Lake Park, Milwaukee, Wisconsin, 1992. 35.5 x 45.5 cm. CCA PH1992:0230

61 "Rockwood Hall," the William D. Rockefeller Estate, Mount Pleasant (Tarrytown), New York, 1994. 35.7 x 45.7 cm. CCA PH1994:0048

62 "The Cedars," the Henry Sargent Hunnewell Estate, Wellesley, Massachusetts, 1994. 35.7 x 45.5 cm. CCA PH1994:0041

63 Highland Park, Rochester, New York, 1991. 35.4 x 45.4 cm. CCA PH1992:0156

64 The Arnold Arboretum, Boston, Massachusetts, 1990. 34.8 x 45.3 cm. CCA PH1991:0178

65 The Arnold Arboretum, Boston, Massachusetts, 1989. 35.1 x 45.2 cm. CCA PH1990:0301

66 The Stone Bridge, Lake Park, Milwaukee, Wisconsin, 1992. 35.5 x 45.5 cm. CCA PH1992:0231

67 Lake Park, Milwaukee, Wisconsin, 1992. 24.1 x 30.3 cm. CCA PH1992:0233

68 "Biltmore," the George W. Vanderbilt Estate, Asheville, North Carolina, 1993. 35.7 x 45.7 cm. CCA PH1993:0350

69 "Biltmore," the George W. Vanderbilt Estate, Asheville, North Carolina, 1990. 25.3 x 32.8 cm. CCA PH1991:0166

Unmounted gelatin silver prints

PAGE 71 The Museum of Science and Industry, Jackson Park, Chicago, Illinois, 1988. 21.7 x 32.8 cm. CCA PH1991:0028

72 (above) The Museum of Science and Industry, Jackson Park, Chicago, Illinois, 1989. 21.7 x 32.9 cm. CCA PH1992:0066

72 (below) The Museum of Science and Industry, Jackson Park, Chicago, Illinois, 1989. 21.7 x 32.8 cm. CCA PH1992:0069

73 (above) The Museum of Science and Industry, Jackson Park, Chicago, Illinois, 1989. 21.6 x 32.8 cm. CCA PH1992:0068

73 (below) The Museum of Science and Industry, Jackson Park, Chicago, Illinois, 1989. 21.7 x 32.8 cm. CCA PH1992:0067

74 Grand Army Plaza, Prospect Park, Brooklyn, New York, 1989. 21.8 x 32.8 cm. CCA PH1991:0044

75 The Maryland Monument, Prospect Park, Brooklyn, New York, 1990. 21.6 x 34.2 cm. CCA PH1992:0098

76 The Agassiz Bridge, the Back Bay Fens, Boston, Massachusetts, 1990. 21.4 x 32.7 cm. CCA PH1992:0183

77 The Pond, the Arnold Arboretum, Boston, Massachusetts, 1990. 21.4 x 32.8 cm. CCA PH1992:0193

78 The Arnold Arboretum, Boston, Massachusetts, 1988. 21.8 x 32.7 cm. CCA PH1991:0002

79 Planter's Hill, World's End, Hingham, Massachusetts, 1991. 21.9 x 33.2 cm. CCA PH1993:0288

80 The Pond, Central Park, New York City, New York, 1991. 21.8 x 32.7 cm. CCA PH1993:0306

81 Riverside Park, New York City, New York, 1991. 21.9 x 33.3 cm. CCA PH1993:0296

82 105th Street, Central Park, New York City, New York, 1993. 26.6 x 25.9 cm. CCA PH1994:0093

83 The Pine Bank Arch, Central Park, New York City, New York, 1994. 26.5 x 25.9 cm. CCA PH1994:0097

84 Morningside Park, New York City, New York, 1990. 21.7 x 32.9 cm. CCA PH1992:0084

85 "Biltmore," the George W. Vanderbilt Estate, Asheville, North Carolina, 1994. 13.9 x 33.5 cm. CCA PH1994:0192

86 The Wilderness, Franklin Park, Boston, Massachusetts, 1991. 21.8 x 33.2 cm. CCA PH1993:0284

87 Fairbank Road, Riverside, Illinois, 1988. 21.7 x 32.6 cm. CCA PH1991:0055

88 Washington Park, Chicago, Illinois, 1992. 26.4 x 25.9 cm. CCA PH1994:0227

89 Shawnee Park, Louisville, Kentucky, 1994. 26.6 x 25.9 cm. CCA PH1994:0213

90 The Arnold Arboretum, Boston, Massachusetts, 1993. 13.9 x 33.5 cm. CCA PH1994:0170

91 Highland Park, Rochester, New York, 1993. 26.6 x 25.9 cm. CCA PH1994:0150

92 Washington Park, Milwaukee, Wisconsin, 1992. 26.4 x 25.9 cm. CCA PH1994:0231

93 "Rockwood Hall," the William D. Rockefeller Estate, Mount Pleasant (Tarrytown), New York, 1992. 37.7 x 37.3 cm. CCA PH1994:0141

OLMSTED ARCHIVE AT THE CCA

Organized chronologically, the following list of sites selected for the CCA commission by Cynthia Zaitzevsky is based on information in *The Master List of Design Projects of the Olmsted Firm, 1857–1950* published by the National Association of Olmsted Parks in 1987. Certain information has been modified as a result of Zaitzevsky's research for the commission. The dates between parentheses indicate work completed by the Olmsted firm after Frederick Law Olmsted's retirement in September 1895.

The numbers following the initials of each photographer (RB, LF, GJ) indicate the number of prints constituting the CCA Olmsted Archive. All photographs were made between 1988 and 1994.

1848–66	*Olmsted Farm*, Staten Island, N.Y.	LF (1), GJ (1)
1857–78 (1935)	*Central Park*, New York, N.Y.	RB (30), LF (55), GJ (44)
1861	*Hillside Cemetery*, Middletown, N.Y.	RB (1), LF (3), GJ (2)
1863–66	*Yosemite Valley and Mariposa Big Tree Grove*, Calif.	LF (4)
1864–66	*Mountain View Cemetery*, Oakland, Calif.	RB (10), LF (22), GJ (10)
1865–95	*Prospect Park*, Brooklyn, N.Y.	RB (24), LF (38), GJ (46)
1866	*Gallaudet College*, Washington, D.C.	LF (1)
1867	*Seaside Park*, Bridgeport, Conn.	LF (4), GJ (2)
1867–86	*Fort Greene Park*, Brooklyn, N.Y.	LF (1)
1868	*Eastern Parkway*, Brooklyn, N.Y.	LF (1)
1868–87	*Riverside*, Riverside, Ill.	RB (7), LF (13), GJ (4)
1868–95 (1915)	*Delaware Park and Buffalo Parkways*, Buffalo, N.Y.	RB (6), LF (4), GJ (5)
1870–71	*Walnut Hill Park*, New Britain, Conn.	RB (2), LF (3)
1870–74	*Ocean Parkway*, Brooklyn, N.Y.	LF (2)
1873–81	*Mount Royal Park*, Montréal, Québec	RB (9), LF (3), GJ (20)
1873–89	*Morningside Park*, New York, N.Y.	LF (17)
	Riverside Park, New York, N.Y.	LF (17), GJ (1)

1874–82	*United States Capitol*, Washington, D.C.	LF (2)
1875–76	*Point Chautauqua*, Mayville, N.Y.	RB (5), LF (1)
1877	*New York State Hospital*, Buffalo, N.Y.	RB (2)
1878–95 (1897)	*Arnold Arboretum*, Boston, Mass.	RB (11), LF (21), GJ (8)
1878–95 (1910)	*Boston Parkways (Arborway and Riverway)*, Boston, Mass.	RB (1)
1878–95 (1920)	*Back Bay Fens*, Boston, Mass.	RB (3), LF (4), GJ (1)
1879–87	*Niagara Reservation*, Niagara Falls, N.Y.	RB (2), LF (7)
1879–87 (1904)	*Schlesinger Estate, "Southwood" (Holy Transfiguration Monastery)*, Brookline, Mass.	RB (1), GJ (4)
1880–81	*Phillips Estate, "Moraine Farm,"* N. Beverly, Mass.	RB (4), GJ (2)
1880–95 (1897)	*Washington Park*, Chicago, Ill.	RB (5), LF (1), GJ (1)
1880–95 (1915)	*Muddy River Improvement*, Boston and Brookline, Mass.	RB (6), LF (13), GJ (10)
1881–83	*Memorial Hall, Oakes Ames Memorial Estate*, N. Easton, Mass.	RB (1), GJ (2)
1882	*Memorial Cairn*, N. Easton, Mass.	RB (1)
1883–93	*Paine Estate, "Stonehurst,"* Waltham, Mass.	RB (1)
1883–95 (1901)	*Lawrenceville School*, Lawrenceville, N.J.	GJ (2)
1883–95 (1955)	*Olmsted Estate, "Fairsted,"* Brookline, Mass.	RB (5), GJ (1)
1884–92	*Fisher Hill Subdivision*, Brookline, Mass.	RB (2)
1885–95 (1921)	*Franklin Park*, Boston, Mass.	RB (12), LF (16), GJ (24)
1886–91	*Planter's Hill and World's End*, Hingham, Mass.	RB (4), LF (11), GJ (8)
1886–93 (1914)	*Stanford University*, Palo Alto, Calif.	RB (3), LF (5)
1886–95 (1899)	*Vanderbilt Mausoleum*, Staten Island, N.Y.	LF (3), GJ (2)
1887–91	*F. L. Ames Estate, "Langwater,"* N. Easton, Mass.	RB (3), GJ (6)
1887–94	*South Park*, Buffalo, N.Y.	LF (1), GJ (2)
1887–95	*W. D. Rockefeller Estate, "Rockwood Hall,"* North Tarrytown, N.Y.	RB (3), LF (11), GJ (10)
1887–95 (1920)	*Downing Memorial Park*, Newburgh, N.Y.	RB (1), LF (10), GJ (2)

1888–92	*Burnham/Adams Estate*, Lincoln, Mass.	RB (1)
1888–95	*H. S. Hunnewell Estate, "The Cedars,"* Wellesley, Mass.	RB (2), GJ (5)
1888–95 (1909)	*G. W. Vanderbilt Estate, "Biltmore,"* Asheville, N.C.	RB (19), LF (21), GJ (19)
1889–91	*Cherokee Park*, Louisville, Ky.	RB (4), LF (14), GJ (17)
1889–94	*Highland Park*, Rochester, N.Y.	RB (1), LF (14), GJ (4)
	Saint Barnabas Church, Falmouth, Maine	GJ (1)
1888–95	*Seneca Park*, Rochester, N.Y.	RB (4)
1891–93	*Oliver Ames III Estate, "Sheep Pasture,"* N. Easton, Mass.	GJ (1)
	Iroquois Park, Louisville, Ky.	RB (1), LF (3), GJ (3)
1891–95 (1929)	*Shawnee Park*, Louisville, Ky.	RB (3), LF (20)
1891–96	*Charlestown Heights*, Boston, Mass.	RB (1), LF (3), GJ (1)
1892	*Lake Park*, Milwaukee, Wis.	RB (6), LF (3)
1892–93	*Washington Square*, Rochester, N.Y.	RB (1), LF (1)
1892–94	*John F. Davis Estate*, St. Louis, Mo.	RB (2)
1892–95	*Washington Park*, Milwaukee, Wis.	RB (2), LF (2)
1892–95 (1900)	*Shore Drive/Bay Ridge Parkway*, Brooklyn, N.Y.	LF (1)
1892–95 (1912)	*Genesee Valley Park*, Rochester, N.Y.	LF (2), GJ (5)
1892–95 (1915)	*Jamaica Park*, Boston, Mass.	RB (6), LF (1), GJ (2)
1892–95 (1921)	*Jackson Park*, Chicago, Ill.	RB (5), LF (16), GJ (3)
1892–1905	*Druid Hills*, Atlanta, Ga.	RB (4), LF (5), GJ (7)
1893–95 (1899)	*Newton Blvd. Syndicate*, Newton, Mass.	RB (2), LF (2)
1893–95 (1903)	*North End Park/Copps Hill Terraces*, Boston, Mass.	RB (1), LF (1)
1893–95 (1915)	*Middlesex Fells*, Metro. Boston, Mass.	LF (3)
1893–95 (1935)	*Charles River*, Metro. Boston, Mass.	LF (6)
1894–95	*Jones, McCormick Residential Estates*, Lake Forest, Ill.	RB (2)
1895	*Pinehurst*, Pinehurst, N.C.	RB (3)